SINK THE BISMARCK!

C. S. FORESTER, an Englishman by parentage, was born in Cairo, Egypt, in 1899, the son of a British Army officer. After service in the infantry in World War I, he began his writing career. In 1937 he wrote the first Horatio Hornblower novel. This would become a series of international bestselling sea adventure novels that would make him one of the most acclaimed writers in the 20th Century. Forester was also the author of *The African Queen* which was made into a movie starring Humphrey Bogart and Katherine Hepburn. Forester moved to the United States in 1940, becoming an American citizen. He died in 1966.

SINK THE BISMARCK!

C. S. FORESTER

Originally published as *The Last Nine Days of the Bismarck*

ibooks

new york
www.ibooks.net
DISTRIBUTED BY SIMON & SCHUSTER

An ibooks, inc. Book

All rights reserved, including the right to reproduce this
book or portions thereof in any form whatsoever.
Distributed by Simon & Schuster, Inc.
1230 Avenue of the Americas, New York, NY 10020

ibooks, inc.
24 West 25th Street
New York, NY 10010

The ibooks World Wide Web Site address is:
http://www.ibooks.net

Originally published as *The Last Nine Days of the Bismarck*

ISBN: 0-7434-5906-7
First ibooks printing June 2003
10 9 8 7 6 5 4 3 2 1

Share your thoughts about *Sink the Bismarck!* and other
ibooks titles in the ibooks virtual reading group at
www.ibooks.net

SINK THE BISMARCK!

Originally published as *The Last Nine Days of the Bismarck*

This is as it may have happened. The speeches are composed by the writer, who has no knowledge that those words were used; but the writer has no doubt that similar speeches were made.

Except in a few places where the truth is not known or where the records are not open to the public, the actual course of events has been recounted; although many of the characters here represented had no actual existence, they at least had their counterparts.

FOREWORD
By
John D. Gresham

"Read the really good books," is my usual answer. The question though is a bit more complex to explain.

For over two decades, I have had the pleasure to be what is known as a "defense analyst." Most folks only encounter such professionals while watching them as "talking heads" on the 24-hour news or documentary film channels. These appearances normally occur during one of the frequent international crises that are the hallmark of our present times. Usually we are asked a few questions by the hosts and try to provide answers that will convey some sort of useful information for the viewers. After that, we normally return to our regular jobs, trying to understand and explain how the military works, and might do better in the future.

A few of us though, get to have a bit more fun. I'm one

of those lucky few.

In 1992, I began to write full-time, something a lifetime of reading had helped prepare me for. This is not to say that every young man or woman who spends his or her adolescence with nose stuck into books is going to become a bestselling author. I was lucky, being knowledgeable in a particular topic (the military) at just the right time (just after the end of the Cold War and Desert Storm). There also is the matter of being a good observer, listener, organizer, and of course, being able to weave what you learn and know into an interesting and accurate story. Just the same, I was very well prepared for both my careers by a lifetime of reading about military history, science, technology, and politics since grade school.

This brings us back to the answer at the beginning of this foreword, since because of the question that I am most frequently asked by people. Everyone usually asks, "How do you become a military analyst and author?" My stock answer of "read the really good books" has a lot more meaning than most of them know though.

It goes without saying that military analysts and authors like myself are voracious readers, consuming a steady diet of e-mail, web newsgroups, and magazines with an ear and eye always cocked to keep watch on a 24-hour television news channel. It is books though, that provide us with the foundations of our knowledge and expertise. Were you to walk into my home, you would find the walls covered with shelves and stacked with books, many acquired decades ago. Some are old friends, dog-eared by continual use. Others stand ready for their days of relevance in some future project. All though, represent the strong base of knowledge that I fall back on time and time again in my work as author, analyst, and citizen.

So what makes a "really good book" that lives on one of *my* bookshelves? That is another insightful question that is also somewhat difficult to answer. "Really good books" always have a timeless quality to them, even when newer volumes have covered or superceded the same subject or time period. Often they form the basis for an examination, or just represent the book interested amateurs should start with. Sometimes these books are just what you feel comfortable recommending to friends and family in the hope that what you offer in advice will not bore or swamp the reader. There is an element of, "I can tell quality when I see it" to these volumes, which brings us to the point of this book and series.

Some months ago, following a truly wonderful experience helping ibooks put out a new edition of the classic book *Zero,* the idea was put forth that perhaps I could provide a list of books that had been of particular significant interest or value to me over the years.

Such lists are quite common actually, with the major service schools and academies around the world all having their own select choices. While each institution has its own particular focus, all share a common desire to provide student readers with a broad and solid foundation of military lessons to take with them into their careers. For example, Robert Heinlein's classic science fiction novel *Starship Troopers* is on *every* American military reading list from the Naval Academy to the Air Force's Air Command and Staff College at Maxwell Air Force Base. *Starship Troopers* encompasses many of the values and virtues desired for good military personnel of all levels, and is a universal favorite. It with this desire to provide civilian readers of military history with a similar background that I began to make up my own reading list for friends, family, and peers.

Thus was born the **John Gresham Military Library**. This series has been designed to give readers a list of books that will allow them to better understand military history from an operational viewpoint, rather than that of grand strategists or national leaders. Battles and campaigns, the real nuts and bolts of a victorious war, are rarely won in national capitols or defense ministries. That duty and honor goes to the soldiers, sailors, airmen, and marines actually in the theaters of war. There is ground truth in such places, where commanding generals and admirals share the elements of personal risk with their subordinates. So expect to see books with a tactical or operational focus in forthcoming volumes.

The subject of the first book in the series is *Sink the Bismarck!* by adventure writer C. S. Forester. Today its hard to remember that in the 1950s the core stories of World War II were just beginning to be told to a public hungry for tales of the conflict. Very few of the details of the *Bismarck* affair were contained in the Admiralty dispatches and press releases of May 1941. Even less was known of what we today call the "back story," including the roles of American lend-lease aircraft and advisors, as well as the breaking of German codes and ciphers. Nevertheless, the story of the *Bismarck* and her nine days of rampage in the North Atlantic were already an obvious source of inspiration for storytellers.

In her day, *Bismarck* was the largest, fastest, most powerful battleship in service. Battleships were still the public measure of seapower in 1941; icons of a dying age where long-range gunnery still determined the fates of nations. While she and her sister ship *Tirpitz* would be superceded by American and Japanese battleship designs later in the war, *Bismarck* was a sea monster of almost unthinkable destructive power in the minds of British naval and political leaders. So impressive were her specifications and so massive her bulk, that her crew and Germany considered *Bismarck* "unsinkable," cursing her with a violent and tragic destiny.

Just months earlier, two smaller and less-well armed German battlecruisers, the *Scharnhorst* and *Gneisenau*, had sunk over 100,000 tons of merchant shipping on just one voyage into the North Atlantic. When *Bismarck* and the heavy cruiser *Prinz Eugen* moved out of the Baltic in May 1941, the worst fears of the British seemed to be coming true. German U-boats and surface raiders were sinking Allied ships faster than yards could replace the losses. Rations of food and other necessities were being reduced throughout England, so heavy were the casualties at sea. Combined with heavy warship losses suffered evacuating Crete following the German airborne invasion, the potential breakout of *Bismarck* and *Prinz Eugen* into the Atlantic convoy routes was the Royal Navy's worst nightmare.

Stretched to the breaking point with commitments around the globe, the Royal Navy was barely able to deal with the menace of *Bismarck*. Unable to cover every possible route into the North Atlantic, the British Home Fleet had to wait for *Bismarck* and *Prinz Eugen* to be found by scouting cruisers before committing itself to the pursuit. What resulted was that most exciting of nautical tales: a sea chase. For over a week *Bismarck* was the center of the greatest such pursuit of World War II. Along the way, she became the centerpiece of a tragic legend.

Initially intercepted in the Denmark Strait between Iceland and Greenland, *Bismarck* stunned the world by sinking the battlecruiser *Hood* and nearly wrecking the new battleship *Prince of Wales.* The loss of *Hood* was particularly galling to the English people, the living symbol of British seapower for over 20 years. Having put two British capital ships out of action and killing over 1,500 seamen in just a single engagement, the Royal Navy spared nothing to bring the German warship to bay. When Prime Minister Winston Churchill gave his famous "sink the *Bismarck*," order to the Royal Navy, it was not just an operational command. It was a demand to avenge the *Hood* and her lost crew.

For days, the *Bismarck* eluded over three dozen British warships trying to run her down. She endured a desperate attack by carrier-based torpedo bombers, one of the first such strikes flown in the war. Then, disappearing into the vile North Atlantic weather, it looked that *Bismarck* would escape the Royal Navy to safe harbor on the coast of occupied France. Only the discovery of *Bismarck* by a Coastal Command PBY Catalina flying boat gave the Royal Navy one final chance to stop her. But the heavy battleships of the Home Fleet were far behind the *Bismarck*, leaving only a handful of "Stringbag" Swordfish torpedo bombers from the aircraft carrier *Ark Royal* to slow her down.

In the fading light of a late spring night, like something out of a *Star Wars* film, one of the Swordfish got a miraculous torpedo hit on the rudders and screws of *Bismarck*. Unable to maneuver away from the oncoming British fleet, *Bismarck* was hounded through her final night by the destroyers of Captain Phillip Vian's flotilla, stalking her until the Home Fleet arrived the next morning. When it came, the *Bismarck's* final battle was little more than a gunnery exercise for the British. Pounded into a floating mass of scrap metal by the battleships *King George V* and *Rodney*, *Bismarck* went down just hours short of the *Luftwaffe* air cover than might have spared her. Only 119 of *Bismarck's* crew of over 2,000 were pulled from the sea after her sinking, one of the worst maritime losses in history. And much like other great ships thought to be "unsinkable," *Titanic* and *Hood* among them, *Bismarck* slipped below the waves to enter the annals of history, legend, and controversy.

Almost immediately following the war, *Bismarck* and her nine-day combat career became the subject of great interest. For example, the means of her final demise is still a matter of bitter dispute. The British claim that torpedoes from the cruiser *Dorsetshire* finished *Bismarck*, while the Germans claim to have used scuttling charges to finish her off. However, much like the doomed ocean liner *Titanic*, *Bismarck's* greatest enduring curiosity was her amazing nine-day combat career. The story of *Bismarck's* one and only combat cruise has been enough to spawn dozens of books, and number documentary and cinematic films. Dr. Robert Ballard led a famous expedition, which located *Bismarck* on the ocean floor in 1989, as well as Academy Award winning producer James Cameron in 2002. Today as then, *Bismarck* is perhaps the most fascinating and compelling warship of World War II.

The 1989 Ballard expedition, his second in search of the

Bismarck, yielded a wealth of information about the German battleship. One of the deepest wrecks ever found and surveyed, *Bismarck* was found upright on the bottom, in surprisingly good shape considering how badly shot up she was by the British. Even a Nazi swastika, painted on the main deck, had survived to be found by Ballard's remote-controlled cameras.

The 2002 Cameron expedition was even more detailed in its examination of the wreck. Using a pair of sophisticated Russian manned submersibles equipped with remote-controlled robotic vehicles, Cameron's team managed to gather a great deal more information. Cameron's cameras obtained a much better damage assessment, including the first conclusive evidence that German scuttling charges were responsible for the final sinking of *Bismarck*. However, the wreck of the *Bismarck* still has many secrets to give up, and future expeditions are probably inevitable. Like the *Titanic, Bismarck* calls to historians, filmmakers, and marine explorers like a siren. The call of the *Bismarck* likely will continue for decades to come.

For now though, let us consider this book, *Sink the Bismarck!* and its author. Most readers under 40 will probably not know the name of Cecil Scott (C.S.) Forester, despite his large and impressive body of work. Prior to his untimely death in 1966, Forester had published dozens of books, along with numerous screenplays and magazine articles. The titles of those books and movies represent a solid piece of our 20th Century culture, and are names many people will know and remember. His *Horatio Hornblower* books are known worldwide, and continue to sell well in new editions four decades after his death. Movies like *The Africa Queen* and *The Pride And The Passion* (originally published in book form as *The Gun*) are considers classics in their own right. Directors including John Houston and Stanley Kramer found his books rich in storylines and characters, making some of their finest films from his fertile tales. These movies provided actors as varied as Gregory Peck, Sophia Loren, Cary Grant, and

Frank Sinatra some of their most memorable performances. In the case of Humphrey Bogart and Katherine Hepburn, Forester's *The African Queen* gave them coveted Academy Awards for what many consider their best work.

In his day C.S. Forester was held in the same esteem as writers like Tom Clancy and Clive Cussler are today. Strangely, his long history of illness (including severe coronary disease) often provided Forester both inspiration and motivation to complete his next project. His sicknesses even brought him to his adoptive home of California, when an assignment to write propaganda film screenplays came his way during World War II. Long before the term "techno-thriller" became a part of pop culture, Forester was churning out a steady stream of adventure novels and popular history books that still have value and resonance today.

Forester had a real sense of craftsmanship when creating characters for his tales, providing readers with a genuine sense of "being there." Sensory experiences as simple as the smells and tastes of food, or the chill of a salt-water shower were just some of the memorable techniques he used to place readers into harm's way for his stories. Like many readers, I have only one real complaint about C.S. Forester, and that was that he ever stopped writing at all. He was working on another *Horatio Hornblower* book at the time of his debilitating stroke in 1964, and clearly had many more wonderful tales in him, if time and health had just allowed. It's a status all authors would like to take to the end of their lives I'm sure.

Interestingly, many people, myself included, consider his "little" books and short stories some of his best work. *Sink the Bismarck!* is one of those thin volumes, and its background is worth some consideration. When released in 1959, *Sink the Bismarck!* (originally published in the United Kingdom and United States respectively as *The Hunt for the Bismarck* and *The Last Nine Days of the Bismarck*) was the first popular telling of the greatest sea chase of World War II. For many people, *Sink the Bismar-*

ck! became the starting point for their first inquiries into the *Bismarck* affair. So great was its appeal to a public hungry for heroic stories in the depths of the Cold War, that the book spawned a popular film (*Sink the Bismarck!* based on the book) and even a Top 40 song.

Now, it needs to be said that *Sink the Bismarck!* is not a history book *per se*. Written as a historical novel rather than a true work of popular history, *Sink the Bismarck!* is a contrivance of Forester's fertile mind asking a simple question.

"What did they do, and what did they say?"

Within the context of the *Bismarck* affair, this was a tougher challenge that most might think in the 1950s. While the basic facts and timetable of the battleships one and only war cruise were part of the record, Forester had little else to work with. None of the senior officers on *Bismarck* survived the sinking, and many British officers and seamen suffered similar fates during World War II.

Prince of Wales, *Ark Royal*, and *Dorsetshire* among others were sunk within a year of *Bismarck*, taking with them the memories of many officers and crewmen. Personal memoirs of the officers and men were still years in the future, as many still served in the armed forces. There was no public knowledge of the Allied codebreaking (ULTRA) which had an important role in the *Bismarck* affair, and nor the covert contributions of American sailors and aircrews who were actively involved with the search for the German battleship. Thus, it was into this vacuum of information and understanding that Forester sought to weave the amazing tale of the *Bismarck* saga into a popular book.

He succeeded through a simple contrivance: Forester made up the dialog out of his personal knowledge of shipboard life. What resulted is the book we know today. *Sink The Bismarck!* is therefore, a somewhat fictionalized account of the Bismarck's pursuit. Nevertheless, it can also be said that the dialog and other more personal scenes in *Sink the Bismarck!* could have taken place as written. In fact, they *probably* did. It is this semblance of authenticity that draws readers in, and introduces them to the real value of *Sink the Bismarck!* That lies in the essential lessons of seapower that are contained in the rich text of the book. Such principals such as reconnaissance and scouting, task organized force mixes, maintenance of fuel and other consumables, along with many other points critical to naval warfare are laid out clearly and simply in *Sink the Bismarck!* Some military professionals go decades without understanding such basic maritime principals. Reading *Sink the Bismarck!* teaches them in just one short reading. Not bad for a thin little book written before most of us even had heard the name *Bismarck*!

It is therefore with no small pride that I launch the **John Gresham Military Library** with a book I have loved since my childhood: *Sink the Bismarck!* I've always had a copy on my bookshelf, and now many others will as well. And if you read *Sink the Bismarck!*, feel your pulse quicken and sense of dread grow, you will begin to know what was felt in the Admiralty just before *Bismarck's* breakout in May 1941. The rest, I have no doubt you will discover on your own as *Sink the Bismarck!* puts you inside the greatest sea chase of World War II. And if when you are finished, you better understand just how "a near run thing" wars sometimes can be, then *Sink the Bismarck!* and C.S. Forester will again have worked their magic on a new generation of readers, in a new century.

John D. Gresham
Fairfax, Virginia
February 2003

This is a story of the most desperate chances, of the loftiest patriotism and of the highest professional skills, of a gamble for the dominion of the world in which human lives were the stakes on the green gaming table of the ocean. There was a pursuit without precedent in the history of navies; there were battles fought in which the defeated gained as much glory as the victors, and in which the most unpredictable bad luck was counterbalanced by miraculous good fortune. For six days that pursuit lasted, days of unrelenting storm, of tossing gray seas and lowering clouds, without a single gleam of sunshine to lighten the setting of the background of tragedy. Those actors in the tragedy who played their parts at sea did so to the unceasing accompaniment of shrieking wind, leaping waves, flying spray, and bitter cold.

And all this took place against a background of events of vital importance in the history of the world, when

England stood alone, almost ringed-in by enemies of unbelievable power and malignity. She was friendless and yet unafraid, guarded and vigilant, although the world's newspapers were pouring from the presses with headlines telling of disasters yesterday and predicting new disasters tomorrow.

BRITAIN'S LAST ALLY CONQUERED, GREECE OVERRUN, said one headline. ATTACK LAUNCHED ON CRETE, said another. JUGOSLAVIA OVERWHELMED . . . . BRITISH IN FULL RETREAT IN NORTH AFRICA . . . . ROMMEL ADVANCES . . . . WILL HITLER MOVE INTO SPAIN NEXT? . . . GERMAN SUBMARINES CLAIM HIGH SUCCESSES IN ATLANTIC . . . . *SCHARNHORST* AND *GNEISENAU* AWAITING THEIR MOMENT IN BREST . . . . BLITZ AGAIN ROCKS ENGLAND . . . .And each succeeding map that the daily papers carried showed how the black stain of Nazi conquest was spreading over frontier after frontier.

Now, at this moment, when Britain's resources and will to survive were being strained to the utmost, preparations were being made to strike another blow against her life-lines. The battleship *Bismarck* was making ready in Gdynia harbor to proceed to sea after a prolonged period of training and working up in the Baltic. The largest, the most dangerous, the most modern ship of war yet launched . . . she was completing her stores, cramming herself as full as her storerooms and her shellrooms and her bunkers would hold. There were meat for her refrigerators and flour and vegetables for her food lockers; oil for her bunkers, fresh water for her tanks, and, above all, shells for her magazines. A fussy little steam train brought up a long train of trucks alongside the ship, each laden with the monstrous fifteen-inch shells, three quarters of a ton each, deadly even in appearance, for the ship's crane to lift and swing into the air, down, down, down, through deck after deck, into the shellrooms far below waterline.

While this was going on a new contingent came marching along the wharf to reinforce—or at least to augment—the ship's company. It was a detachment of young naval officers, very young indeed, hardly more than boys. They were newly promoted cadets—proud of their new status and of their new uniforms—swinging briskly and proudly in formation to the gangway leading down from the ship's side; the band, which had preceded them so far, halted at the foot and continued to play as the young men turned with military precision to march up the gangway; as they reached the quarterdeck, the senior officer saluted the officer of the watch and reported the arrival of his party on board. A word of command brought them into formation facing the bridge at the moment when the work on the dockside was completed.

The officer on the dock supervising the loading of the ammunition shouted, "Last one!"

"Last one," echoed the officer on the deck, waving one finger in reply to the finger waved to him. The last fifteen-inch shell, grim and ugly, swung up in the crane to make its descent into the shellroom. The busy gangs of workers on the dockside melted away; the band, still playing, marched off towards the gate, its music dying away slowly. Only the sailors standing by the lines remained, apparently. Admiral Lutjens, brisk, efficient, and active, came out of his sea cabin and made his way to the loud-speaker on the bridge.

"Gentlemen!" he began his speech, as the young officers stiffened to attention to hear him, listening enthralled. The words he uttered were carried throughout the ship by the public-address system. He welcomed the young officers aboard, and he explained to them that they had been expressly detailed by the highest authority to make this voyage, so that on their return they would disseminate through the Navy the details of the triumphs they had witnessed. They were in the newest and most powerful battleship afloat, and they were going to experience high adventure. There was no ship in the British Navy that could face them in single combat; there was no large ship that could escape them. Four months of harsh training in the Baltic had made the *Bismarck* the most efficient ship in the world. Did British convoys cover the Atlantic? *Bismarck* could make short work of convoys and escorts, with the aid of the *Prinz Eugen*, accompanying them on this voyage of honor. The *Queen Elizabeth* and the *Queen Mary,* the pride of Britain, were crossing the Atlantic over and over again without escort, relying on their speed. *Bismarck* was faster than they. What would the world say when the news came of the sinking of the *Queen Mary* with ten thousand troops on board? One or two blows like that, and England would not dare to send a merchant ship to sea. For as long as *Bismarck* could maintain herself in the Atlantic, England's commerce would be disrupted; and the British people, shattered and shaken already by the blitz, would starve. He had already ranged the whole length of the Atlantic in command of the battle cruisers *Scharnhorst* and *Gneisenau,* and had sunk a quarter of a million tons of British shipping. A quarter of a million tons . . . . Now they could set themselves a target of two million tons, dealing a blow from which England could never recover. . . .

Down on the dockside one last worker was lingering over some remains of his job, half hidden by piles of stores. The sound of the speech, conveyed over the loud-speaker, just reached his ears. He heard those words about the Atlantic, about the *Queen Mary*. With the last words of the speech he sauntered down the dock, with every appearance of innocence. His papers were quite in order as he showed them to the police. Already sailors at the lines were singling up and then casting off. *Bismarck* swung herself about and headed out to sea; the dockyard workers massed at the gate watched her go, and the band played.

At a small port in Sweden a long pier ran out to sea, and on it someone in civilian clothes was quietly fishing. He was surrounded by proof of how closely Sweden guarded her neutrality, how much she feared a surprise attack—Swedish soldiers and Swedish coast-guardsmen were constantly patrolling and gazing out to sea. He sat there endlessly, leisurely eating his lunch, changing his bait and occasionally securing a fish. The sun was setting and the Northern day nearly at an end when, looking southward, he saw something silhouetted against the remaining glow in the sky. He had binoculars hanging round his neck; he whipped them to his eyes, gazed long and carefully, rested his eyes, and gazed again. There was no mistaking what he saw: two almost identical silhouettes, one large and one small; the *Bismarck* and the *Prinz Eugen* with a crowd of merchant ships—eleven all told—accompanying them. He dismantled his fishing rod, picked up his gear, and hurried shoreward along the pier, through the Swedish guards, into the main street, past the post office.

It was into that post office, a few minutes later, that an elderly Englishman came striding. He filled out a telegraph form with a few rapid words and handed it over the counter; the girl there read the address and summoned a waiting Swedish policeman with her eyes. He came up and began questioning. The address was that of a London company in Cheapside; the message said: PIT PROPS AND BATTENS RISING. ELEVEN POINTS AT LEAST—NO MORE.

"What is this firm?" asked the policeman.

"Timber importers—everyone knows them."

"What does this message say?"

The Englishman satisfied his questioner, showed his papers, and a nod from the policeman allowed the message to be sent with a small apology: "Our country has to make sure her neutrality is not violated, you understand, sir."

In a London telegraph office the keys began to chatter as a message came through. A girl dealt with it in the ordinary routine manner, but a supervisor noticed the address.

"Just a minute," she said with a hurried reference to a file, running her finger down a list.

* * *

A moment later a motorcyclist was roaring through the blitzed streets of London. He dismounted at the Admiralty and delivered the message. It passed rapidly from hand to hand until it reached a rear admiral. The clock showed eight o'clock in the morning; the calendar showed May 21, 1941. There it was. PIT PROPS AND BATTENS RISING. He looked at the chart of the Baltic beside him on the wall, identified the town of origin—Malmo—and flipped through a code book.

"Well," he said to a colleague. "*Bismarck*'s on the move. Heading north in the Kattegat. Here."

He pointed to the chart.

"She's been exercising in the Baltic for four months," said his colleague. "It's about time we heard from her."

"*Prinz Eugen*'s with her," said the rear admiral, still referring to his list. "And eleven merchant ships."

"It could be something very big indeed."

"I'll take it along this minute."

An admiral was in the War Room when the rear admiral

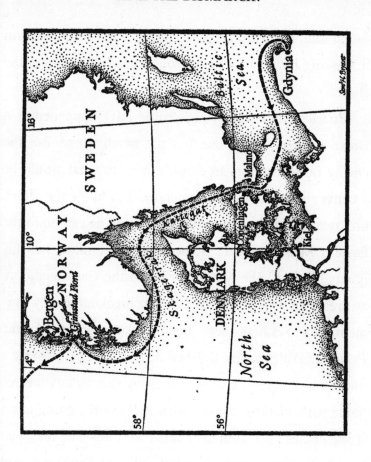

Map 1

"Bismarck's on the move. Heading north . . ."

found him. He heard the news and began to comment on it, moving his pencil slowly from point to point over the chart.

"*Bismarck* moving . . . . It could have happened at a worse moment, I suppose, but not much worse. But the enemy never troubles to consult us as to what would be a convenient time for us, somehow. You know the attack on Crete has begun? Cunningham has all he can do in the Eastern Mediterranean. Somerville at Gibraltar has his hands full, too. The *Scharnhorst* and the *Gneissenau* are at Brest; we have to watch for their breakout at any moment. Convoys here—here—here . . . All over the Atlantic. *Prince of Wales* hasn't finished her training yet. Not by a long shot. You can't call her a fighting ship by any means. Same with *Victorious*. And what is *Bismarck* going to do if she comes out? Merchant ships with her—she may just be convoying them to Norway. But—we have to guard against every move. There's the Faeroes. There's Iceland. I wouldn't like an attack upon either at present—it would hurt. And supposing he's going to break out into the Atlantic? Which route? Pentland Firth? Fair Isle? East of the Faeroes? West of the Faeroes? Denmark Strait? Which? A thousand miles of water go guard, and precious few ships to do it with . . . "

"And not one as dangerous as the *Bismarck,* sir," said the rear admiral.

"That's something I don't need reminding about." The admiral led the way into his own office. "Anyway, put Coastal Command to work. I want air reconnaissance of the Norwegian coast. I was photographs. That telegram's eight hours old now. She could be"—the dividers turned in a circle over the chart—"anywhere from Bergen southward. Photographs fo anything suspicious from Bergen, Oslo Fiord, and south from there."

I'll tell Coastal Command, sir."

It was now nine o'clock.

The reconnaissance Spitfires roared off on their mission,

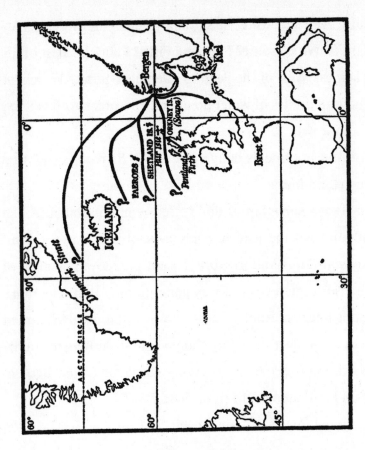

Map 2

"Which route?"

searching the whole tangled coast of southern Norway. The pilot of one of them thought he saw something in Grimstad Fiord south of Bergen, circled, made sure of what he was looking at, and photographed it. He noted the time on his wrist watch—1:15. Then he headed for home. On board the *Bismarck* they had seen his coming on their radar, and had turned out to man the guns, the young supernumerary officers eagerly standing to see the action, but there was only time to recognize the type—SCHPIT-FEUER—before she was gone again.

The pilot landed and climbed out of his plane. "Two cruisers in Grimstad Fiord," were his first words to the eager people who greeted him. They seized his camera and hastened off with it. Steady hands took out the film, developed it, printed it, and enlarged the prints—with the hands of the clock creeping along all the time. He had landed at 2:45. It was 3:15 by the time the enlargements were in the hands of experts.

"Two cruisers!" said one of them. "No, that's the *Bismarck* and the *Prinz Eugen*."

Telephones began to buzz.

"*Bismarck* in Grimstad Fiord!"

Someone in the Admiralty received the news; his clock showed 3:45.

"We've been lucky," he said. "We saw her off Sweden and now we've found her in Norway. We'll have bombers over her by six o'clock."

"Lucky!" said the man he addressed. "Look at this."

It was a meteorological report from the Orkneys, to the effect that mist and rain were closing in and visibility deteriorating rapidly.

"By six o'clock it will be all shut down. They'll never find her. Don't you ever say we're lucky again. That's the unluckiest thing to say there ever was. Lucky!"

So it was to prove. The reports began to come in as the hands of the clock turned on to midnight and beyond, as someone tore off the sheet showing May 21 on the calendar to reveal May 22.

"No luck." "No luck." "Cloud down to 100 feet." "Visibility nil." "Couldn't see a thing."

Exhausted R.A.F. pilots said these things to the officers who questioned them.

Meanwhile, at midnight, a German naval officer came into the day cabin of Admiral Lutjens; the admiral was dozing in an armchair, his head propped on his hand.

"Meteorological forecast, sir," said the officer.

Lutjens was immediately awake.

"Call the captain," he said after a glance at the paper, and then, on the captain's arrival: "Here's the forecast. Two days of thick weather at least . . . Now's the time. I want to be out of here in ten minutes."

"Aye aye, sir," said the captain.

Bismarck was in the second degreed of readiness, with the AA guns manned. In the hardly relieved darkness on deck could just be seen the men at their stations, with the mist swirling round them in wreaths. Below decks half the ship's company was sleeping, or trying to, when at this moment the loud-speaker began to blare, giving orders for the anchor parties to go to their stations, and all hands to their posts. There was immediate orderly bustle as the men tumbled out, the supernumerary officers in a state of great excitement. A shaded lamp was flickering a message to the *Eugen*; there was an acknowledgment. The capstans began to turn, the dripping cables came in link by link, messages passed back and forward from forecastle to bridge; the engines began to turn, the propellers turned with them, and the huge ship gradually got under way and moved ponderously along through the swirling mist.

It was at this time that, through the blacked-out streets of London, a motorcyclist was picking his way as hurriedly as he could manage, to deliver his message, as before, to the Admiralty, and it passed, as before, to the rear admiral. It looked like an ordinary letter, but it was read with extreme care, and with constant reference to code books. Soon the rear admiral was hastening to the admiral with his news.

"Here's something that looks important, sir. About the *Bismarck*."

"Well?"

"It's about four days old, sir; but from our contact in Gdynia dockyard, and it had to come through Switzerland and Portugal."

"I didn't know you had a contact in Gdynia dockyard."

"The fewer people who know that the better, sir. We don't hear from him often—he daren't risk getting into touch too often, as you can guess, sir. But he's good—he's never failed us yet."

"What does he say?"

"He says *Bismarck*'s going to try to break out into the Atlantic, sir. He says he's quite positive about it. Got his information from the admiral, from Lutjens himself."

"Nonsense."

"I'd be surprised if it were, sir."

"You say this fellow's good?"

"One of the best we've got, sir. He's never let us down so far."

"Not easy to believe."

"I'd bet money on him, sir."

"Maybe. But now you're betting your job and any credit you have in the Navy. And I might point out that it's not only your job that depends on this. It's victory or defeat—the safety of this country. Now what do you say?"

There was only a momentary hesitation before the reply came.

"I'd go ahead, sir. I think this fellow's got something."

"Very well." The admiral picked up the telephone. "Get me the Chief of Staff, Flagship Home Fleet."

As he waited for the connection to be made his eye roamed over the chart he had been looking at earlier in the day.

"Maybe your information's as good as you say, But that

doesn't make it any less than a thousand miles of sea to guard—it hasn't grown any narrower since this morning."

There was a telephone wire running north from the Admiralty, running for five hundred miles overland to the extreme north of Scotland, dipping down into the stormy Pentland Firth, winding its way to Scapa Flow, climbing up to a buoy there, and extending from there to the Fleet flagship as she rode to the buoy in the Flow. It ascended into the ship and down again to the switchboard below water. The seaman operating the switchboard there saw the glow of the light, heard who was calling ashore, and plugged in. Meanwhile the admiral had been passing time with a comment or two.

"I'm not going to give orders—I'm not even going to offer advice. The Commander in Chief knows his business as well as I do, and he knows his subordinates better. It'll be up to him. I'll give him this extra information for what it's worth. I don't worry him much. There's a direct line between him and me—leakproof, spyproof, ideal for confidential chats—and yet I don't use it."

The telephone rang sharply and he picked it up.

"Chief of Staff? Here's a scrap of additional information come in from Intelligence. This Lutjens fellow in the *Bismarck* apparently told someone before he sailed that he was destined for the Atlantic . . . . Yes, it sounds like it, doesn't it, but the rear admiral swears it's true. It's worth bearing in mind—I'll send you the details in writing tonight. The Commander in Chief can act as he thinks proper . . . . Yes, you've just comfortable time to cover the Denmark Strait . . . . I quite agree . . . . Very well. Goodby."

He put down the telephone and addressed himself to the rear admiral again.

"With the weather closed down like this, *Bismarck*'ll probably move at once, to take advantage of it. If she does better than 25 knots Tovey will have to act this minute, or she'll be through Denmark Strait and the fox will be among the chickens."

"If she takes that route, sir."

"Yes." The admiral's pencil wandered over the chart. "There are plenty of other routes, and Tovey has to guard them all. He'll probably cover the other exits himself and send *Hood* and *Prince of Wales* on ahead."

"An old lady and a little boy, sir," said the rear admiral.

"The old lady ought to be a fighting termagant. And the little boy may have grown up by now, let's hope. There's nothing else to spare, anyway. Between them, this ought to stop him."

"A bandit with a bludgeon," said the rear admiral.

They walked back into the War Room, and stood among the bustle and busy-ness. Telephones rang and messages dropped down tubes. A WREN officer approached the chart and made an alteration to it in the neighborhood of Scapa. The admiral looked at it.

"They're off," he said.

In the utter misty darkness of Scapa Flow, signal lamps

began to flicker, calling and answering. There was a clatter of boots on still decks. A squawking of telephones in the darkness. A voice into a speaking tube . . .

"Captain, sir, signal from the flag—"

Down below on the mess decks the loud-speaker shrilled with the noise of the pipe of the bosun's mate. *"Call the port watch. Cable party muster on the forecastle in ten minutes. Call the watch."* The immense mess deck was packed fullof hammocks slung at every possible point, out of which men began to slide sleepily.

"What's the flap about?" asked someone.

"Just call up the admiral and ask him," said someone else. "I've got to go and get that anchor up."

"Hope it keeps fine for you," said another. The man he was addressing was putting on sea boots and reaching for his oilskins, among the tremendous jam of belongings packed everywhere, illustrating the extreme of crowding in which the men lived.

"What are you dressing up for, Nobby?" asked someone.

"Didn't your invite say evening dress optional?"

"'E thinks 'e's on the sunny Riviera," said another.

Nobby was now in sea boots and oilskins.

"Make way for a man who's got a man's work to do," he said, pushing through the crowd. He went clattering forward through the vast ship, along alleyways and up ladders, with methodical bustle all round him. He emerged from the bright lights onto the forecastle; in the darkness there, other oilskins gleamed faintly. Rain was driving across the forecastle, and a wind was persistently wailing as they went about their business of weighing anchor.

Down in a dark cabin a telephone squawked, and although a light was instantly turned on it squawked again before the tousled man in the bunk reached for it.

"Commander E."

"*Steam in ten minutes, sir,*" squawked the telephone.

"Right. I'm coming," said the engineer commander, plunging out of bed and reaching for his uniform.

It was an exact repetition of what was going on in the

Bismarck at that very moment; the clocks in the two brightly lit engine rooms exactly coincided, at twenty minutes past midnight. The capstan turned, the cable came in link by link, the messages passed back and forth, the valves were opened to admit steam to the turbines, the propellers began to revolve in the dark water, and the ship, with signals still flashing from her shaded lamps, began slowly to move out of Scapa Flow through the outer submarine defenses. It might have been the *Bismarck* all over again, except that the faint light illuminated her name, *Hood,* upon her stern. So at the same moment the two ships set out, *Bismarck* reaching far into the north to pass round Iceland, *Hood,* with *Prince of Wales* following her, plowing along on a more southerly course to intercept *Bismarck* in Denmark Strait if she were heading that way. And the moment *Prince of Wales* left the sheltered waters of the Flow, the storm awaited her. Up rose her bows and then down again, up and down, as the spray flew in great sheets aft to the bridge.

Bismarck was meeting the same conditions, or worse; she was plowing over mountains of icy gray water, lifting and heaving. Moreover, now she was at sea, and at sea every man's hand was against her; there was no chance of her meeting a friend, and there was every chance of her meeting an enemy. Admiral Lutjens and Captain Lindemann were discussing this very point over cigars in the captain's sea cabin immediately under the bridge, which was heaving and swaying with the ship's motion.

"But as far as the enemy knows, sir," said Lindemann, "we are still in Grimstad Fiord. They have no certain knowledge that we are at sea; and if they had, they'd have no means of guessing what course we're steering."

"My dear Lindemann, look at the other side of the matter. The sea is theirs, all theirs—we are furtive trespassers. Let's face it. That's what we are, at present, even if we are destined to reverse that state of affairs in a few more months. How can you be sure that a British ship of war won't appear under our bows at any moment—now, this minute, or in five minutes' time?"

"Our Intelligence—"

"Our Intelligence makes mistakes, and you know it, Captain. What's the visibility? Two miles? More like one mile. Our radar's unsure. We'd have no warning before we were under fire. We must be ready at *any* moment to blow *any* enemy out of the water before he has the chance to inflict *any* injury on us."

"But we're going to be at sea a long time, sir. After a few days the men will be worn out."

"After a few days we may be able to relax. Meanwhile my order stands. Every man at his station. Half of them can sleep, but let no man leave his post."

"Very well, Admiral."

So that was the situation in the *Bismarck*. In the crowded turrets, down in the shellrooms and handling rooms, in the engine rooms and boiler rooms, the whole ship's complement was present. Half the men attended to their duty; the other half rested how and where they could. Lucky ones could lie down, often curling themselves, perforce, round projections in the decks. Others sat leaning against bulkheads, swaying with the motion of the ship, and being jerked back into wakefulness by an unexpected heave.

"It is part of the price we pay for not being masters of the sea, Captain," said Lutjens. "We can remember that, when the time comes when England asks for peace."

"I understand, sir," said Lindemannn. To change the subject he asked a question into a voice-pipe and listened to the answer, which he relayed to Lutjens. "Visibility considerably less than one mile, Admiral."

Even stronger words were being used in the Admiralty, where an officer was reporting to the admiral.

"Visibility absolutely nil, sir. Not a hope of seeing anything in Grimstad Fiord."

"M'm," said the admiral. "She was sighted at one P.M. yesterday. Now it's"—he looked at clock and calendar—"twelve noon today. Twenty-three hours. What's her 'farthest on'?"

The officer swung his dividers in a wide arc centering on Grimstad.

"That's it, sir. At 25 knots. Say six hundred miles. She could be anywhere within that circle."

"Or she could still be in Grimstad while we make fools of ourselves. Ask Coastal Command to try again."

"Aye aye, sir. There's some of the Fleet Air Arm at Hatston"—the officer indicated the position of the airfield near Scapa Flow—"with bags of experience of this sort of thing. They're bursting to have a go, sir."

"Let 'em try. Fix it up with Coastal Command."

It was a Maryland bomber which took off from Hatston in the afternoon. It had a perilous flight. The clouds hung low over the sea, and yet to estimate the force of the wind on the plane the pilot had to come down within sight of

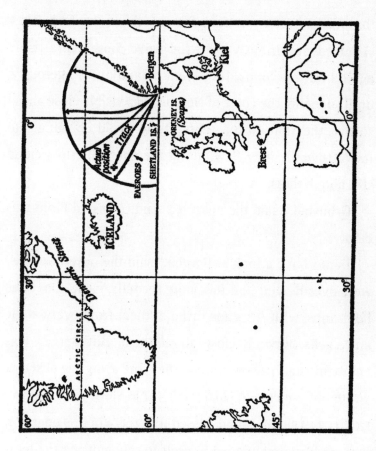

Map 3

"She could be anywhere within that circle."

the waves—within a few feet of them, in fact. They skimmed precariously over the wave-tops before rising again into the clouds. They went on and on, dangerously, until suddenly the coast of Norway was visible close ahead so that they had to turn abruptly to avoid crashing into it. Northwards they flew, along the coast, the low cloud still above them.

"Grimstad," said the observer. And Grimstad Fiord was empty.

"Better have a look at Bergen," said the observer. They were over Bergen in a few more seconds, close above the housetops, with AA guns firing at them from every angle and shells bursting close about them. But Bergen was empty of ships of war, too. As they tore away the observer wrote out a message—*Bismarck* NOT IN SIGHT IN GRAMSTAD FIORD OR IN BERGEN—and passed it to the wireless operator, who nodded and applied himself to transmitting the message as the plane flew back homewards through the clouds.

SINK THE BISMARCK!

It was seven o'clock by the operator's watch.

It was 7:15 when the message reached the War Room.

"So the bird's flown," said the admiral. "Thirty hours since the last sighting. What's their 'farthest on' now?"

The officer drew a much larger arc on the chart.

"Seven hundred and fifty miles, sir. There it is."

"Just as well *Hood* left last night," was the admiral's comment. "*Bismarck* might be—" He drew with his pencil a series of possible courses for the *Bismarck*, in each case ending the line at the outer circle. "She might for that matter be—" He drew with his pencil a series of possible courses for the *Bismarck*, in each case ending the line at the outer circle. "She might for that matter be—HERE, or HERE." He indicated a course back into the Baltic and then through the Kiel Canal. "In that case we'll have burned up forty thousand tons of oil for nothing—forty thousand tons? More like sixty thousand—and we'll have given say twenty thousand men a free trip to sea. That is, if the rest of the Home Fleet leaves Scapa, and it's beginning to look as if it should."

A message clattered down one of the tubes, and a copy of it was handed to him.

"Yes," he said, passing it over to his staff. "Tovey thinks the same. He's going to sea. Plenty of exits to guard against besides Denmark Strait. He'll have *King George V, Repulse, Victorious.* Enough to do his business for him, if *Bismarck* comes his way."

It was while the admiral was speaking that the Home Fleet was making preparations to go to sea. And at the same time, Lutjens and Lindemann and various staff officers were gathered in the operations room in *Bismarck*; on the chart table before them lay a chart of the northern waters with *Bismarck*'s track up to now marked upon it.

"I still fail to see the need to go as far as Denmark Strait, sir," said Lindemann. "The other passages are nearer and far wider. We could turn now."

"Visibility's still bad, sir," added a staff officer.

A glance outside showed that this was the truth. Almost nothing could be seen of any horizon, as *Bismarck* heaved and tossed upon a rough gray sea.

"There'll be cruisers patrolling all of the passages," said another staff officer. "Even if nothing can fly."

"The U-boats' last report gives the ice from Greenland stretching within sixty miles of Iceland," said another. "Then there are the minefields on the other side. One cruiser can watch a twenty-mile channel even in thick weather." A message clattered down the tube as they were speaking; a staff officer opened it and handed it to the chief of staff.

"From Berlin, sir," announced the latter. "A British reconnaissance plane flew over Grimstad and Bergen at 7:00 P.M. Visibility was temporarily good, and they could undoubtedly see we had left."

All eyes looked at the clock and then at the chart. The chief of staff picked up the dividers.

"They saw us yesterday in Grimstad at one. Thirty hours

ago. We left at midnight. For all they know we could be HERE"—two hundred and fifty miles farther along—"or we might only be HERE"—marking a spot a short distance from the Norwegian coast—"while actually we are HERE ."

"Yes," said Lutjens, nodding his head over the chart. "No information about British movements?"

"No, sir. Hard to get information from England. And visibility has been as bad for our planes as for theirs."

"I can't believe the English would move before they got this news," said Lutjens, tapping the message. "Their Home Fleet was all in British waters by our last information. They'll start moving now, perhaps. They'll never reach Denmark Strait in time, but they *could* intercept us HERE, in the neighborhood of the Faeroes. So it is my order that we head for Denmark Strait. We may meet a cruiser, but we'll brush her aside."

"Very well, sir."

H.M.S. *Suffolk* and H.M.S. *Norfolk* were patrolling in

Denmark Strait. By the invisible sun it was late afternoon—the westerly sky was already faintly pink in the thin
mist. It was an utterly dreary scene. To the west lay the
ice, humped and jagged as far as the eye could see. To the
east there was fog, impenetrable to the eye. A perpetual
cold wind was shrieking along the deck, and the ships
were rolling deeply in the heavy swell. The lookouts sat
at their posts, the binoculars to their eyes, all round the
bridge, sweeping steadily from side to side, and then up
and down, turning back and forward in their swivel chairs.
Other groups of muffled-up men stood seeking what little
shelter there was beside the AA guns; occasional sheets
of spray sweeping the decks as the ship put her shoulder
into a wave added to their discomfort.

On the *Suffolk*, the squeal of the pipe of the bosun's
mate came over the public-address system.

"*Captain speaking. We've had some news from home.
The German battleship* Bismarck *is out, with the cruiser*
Eugen. *All we know is that she's somewhere to the north*

of Iceland. The weather's too thick for any plane to spot her. But we can be sure she's not going to stop where she is. She'll be coming south. And more likely than not—very much more likely than not—she'll be coming this way, down Denmark Strait. She'll be coming at twenty-five knots or more when she comes, too . . . . It'll be our job to spot her and report her to the Admiralty. In case you've forgotten, I'll remind you that she has fifteen-inch guns and can hit us at fifteen miles. That's why you're at action stations, and that's why the lookouts have been doubled. If any man were not to do his duty he would be imperiling the ship and the lives of all his shipmates. I know you'll do your duty without that reminder."

"Fifteen-inchers! Keep your eyes skinned, Dusty," one of the men at the AA guns called ot one of the lookouts.

"And you can try keeping your trap shut," muttered Dusty, not hesitating for a moment in his eternal swinging backward and forward with binoculars and chair. "If 'e's there to be seen I'll see 'im."

The cruisers continued to patrol in the icy wind over the heaving sea, between the ice and the fog.

"There are matelots at 'ome," said one of the group on deck, "'oo 'ave warm billets. Just think of that. Blokes who've forgotten what it's like to be cold."

In the War Room things were comparatively quiet. Only the minimum of messages was coming through; there was no bustle or excitement. The rear admiral was entertaining an air vice marshal, a big beefy man with an Air Force mustache.

"I don't doubt you find it the same in the Air Force," said the rear admiral, "but in the Navy we're inclined to say it about our war experience in all ranks: Long periods of waiting for something to happen, and then much too much to do all of a sudden. No moderation either way."

"Oh yes, yes, yes," gobbled the air vice marshal. "I suppose we can say the same."

"Of course, over there," said the rear admiral, pointing to another part of the room, "they're fighting a real war. Never a dull moment for *them*. All hell has broken loose on Crete. So they've gone off on their own with the Eastern Mediterranean and left us to look after the *Bismarck* and the North Atlantic. And you can see how quiet it is at present."

"Yes, yes, yes," gobbled the air vice marshal.

"If your fellows could only get into the air," said the rear admiral with a sweep of his hand over the northern part of the chart, "we might not feel the period of waiting so acutely."

"Visibility's still nil there. What's the situation as far as you know?"

"Let's have a chart and I'll show you," said the rear admiral.

The WREN officer came to make a change on the big war map.

"What's that?" asked the rear admiral sharply.

"Just a convoy, sir."

"Very well." The rear admiral had a black crayon in his hand and he began making sweeping lines on the chart with it. "Here are two possible courses for the *Bismarck*. Perhaps the most likely ones. At her highest practical speed, she'll be somewhere between HERE and HERE, or between HERE and HERE. That's the best we can do about her."

"Yes."

"*Hood* and *Prince of Wales* sailed from Scapa two nights ago. Forty-three hours ago. They'll be somewhere HERE."

"Can't you be sure?"

"No. They are maintaining wireless silence. So's *Bismarck*, as you can guess. We've cruisers trying to watch the gaps as well as they can in the thick weather. *Arethusa* and *Manchester*, HERE between the Faeroes and Iceland, and two HERE in the Denmark Strait. You can see for yourself why we've been screaming for air patrols."

41

During this speech the rear admiral had looked, over and over again, anxiously at the officers and ratings who were receiving messages down the tubes. Each time he had been disappointed by a shake of the head.

"And what do you think's going to happen?" asked the air vice marshal.

"I'm sure *Bismarck*'ll have a try for it. Maybe HERE, maybe THERE." The rear admiral's crayon drew two black lines, continuing the ones he had already drawn. Then from the *Hood*'s position he drew two more diverging lines, heading to meet the two lines for the *Bismarck*. "*Hood*'ll take one course or the other, according to the cruiser reports. And that's where they'll meet. THERE or THERE."

He indicated points east and west of Iceland.

"And then the balloon goes up, what?" said the air vice marshal.

"It's time we heard from those cruisers," said the rear

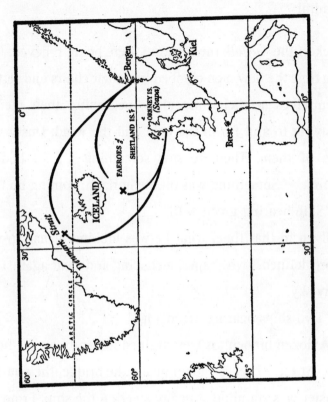

Map 4

"*Hood*'ll take one course or the other . . . And that's where they'll meet. THERE or THERE."

admiral.

Back in the *Suffolk* the lookouts were being relieved. One at a time the new men climbed into their chairs and settled themselves at their binoculars, beginning their eternal swaying to and fro in the cold and the wind. Dusty was one of them. Then he saw something . . . . Looked again . . . .Something was on the horizon, coming up fast.

"Ship bearing green 140!"

Even in that time, what he was looking at had grown more defined. Two shapes, menacing and clear against the gray sky.

"Two ships bearing green 140!"

A dozen binoculars were trained instantly on the bearing. At the wheel far down below the bridge, the quartermaster was standing stoically steering the ship. From the voice-pipe over his head came the sharp order. "*Hard a-port!*" He swung the wheel over frantically. The ship heeled with the violence of her turn. Round she came—the two objects in Dusty's binoculars swung away out of his field of vision.

"Signal to Admiralty," said a voice on the bridge . . . ."most immediate: *Bismarck* AND CRUISER IN SIGHT. ENEMY'S COURSE SOUTH. MY POSITION . . . give the latitude and longitude."

"As long as she doesn't hit us before we get that message off," said another voice.

"Here's the fog," said another. "Ah!"

Suffolk dashed into the fog as though into a wall. It came swirling back from the bows, round the bridge, and enveloped the stern; in ten seconds she was completely invisible in the dripping mist, still heeling with her extreme turn, her wake boiling behind her, Dusty and the others still at their posts in disciplined stillness.

"*Steer one-eight-o,*" said the voice down the voice-pipe to the quartermaster.

Meanwhile the signal that had been dictated was going

its way, down to the coding officer and then along to the wireless transmitter. It rattled and chattered, sending the news round the world.

In the War Room a junior officer turned to the rear admiral.

"Most immediate message coming through, sir."

"Let's have it."

Those were long seconds of waiting as the rear admiral and the air vice marshal fidgeted at the chart. Now it came rattling down the tube; it seemed hours as the officer fumbled it open, hours more as the rear admiral read it.

"It's all right," he said. "They've found her. *Suffolk* is shadowing her, in Denmark Strait. Latitude . . . Longitude . . . " referred to the message. "HERE."

Somebody gave a cheer. Every face was smiling.

"So that's it," said the air vice marshal, pointing with his stick to one of the alternative courses for *Hood*. "This is where they'll meet, eh?"

"Yes," said the rear admiral—a little more grave than the others.

"What's worrying you?" asked the air vice marshal.

"Things can still go wrong. *Hood*'s an old lady now, a very old lady. She's twenty years older than *Bismarck*. Do you remember the planes of 1920, sir? How would you like to fight a new Messerschmitt in a Farman biplane?"

"But there's this other one—what's her name—*Prince of Wales*?"

"And she's too young, sir. No time to work up the ship's company, no time to cure her teething troubles. She hasn't been completed a month. You might say she's still in the builder's hands. I know she's gone to sea with the contractor's workmen still on board."

"That'll be an experience for 'em."

"They'll be fighting a battle in their little bowler hats."

The officer receiving messages came with another.

"Position, course and speed, sir," he said.

The admiral was in the War Room now. The change in

atmosphere was very apparent. There was excitement, but it was (except for the rear admiral) confident, almost pleasurable excitement. Signals were being sent off in numbers: "SIGNAL FOR THE COMMANDER IN CHIEF, *King George V.*

"SIGNAL FOR *Rodney.*"

"SIGNAL FOR *Ramillies.*"

The admiral was addressing the air vice marshal.

"Get your chaps to do all they can to cover the Strait," he said.

"Yes, sir," said the air vice marshal. "Visibility's still bad, sir."

"I know. But now you can explain to them how urgent it is. You're up to date on the situation. Somewhere HERE, about dawn tomorrow."

The admiral indicated a spot on the chart to the southward of Denmark Strait.

In the operations room of the *Hood* the admiral and his

staff were bent over a similar chart. Someone was working on it with ruler and dividers. "The intercepting course is 310°, sir," said the navigating officer. "You can expect contact any time after 0200."

"I don't want to engage until daylight. Give me a course and speed to intercept an hour before sunrise."

Ruler and dividers went to work again. One line went to meet another.

"At 27 knots, sir, course 295°, we shall meet at dawn, HERE."

The pencil made a black cross—a significant mark—on the chart where the two lines met.

"Very well. You can inform the ship's company, Captain. And"—to the chief of staff—"pass all this news on to *Prince of Wales*."

At a gesture from the captain, the bosun's mate outside the operations room shrilled with his pipe into the loud-speaker, and the captain began to speak.

"Captain speaking . . . "

Down in the incredibly crowded mess deck the watch below were taking their ease as well as they could.

"We don't know where we're going but we're on our way," said someone. All the hanging garments down there were swaying rhythmically to and fro with the movement of the ship.

"You always want to know where you're going, Nobby," said someone else. "Can't you ever be satisfied?"

"I know where we're not going," said someone else, "and that's south. Who'd like a spell of the tropics?"

"It's snowing outside, they tell me. Who wouldn't sell a farm and go to sea?"

This was when they heard the bosun's mate's pipe and the captain's voice:

"Captain speaking. Here's the news. The Bismarck *is out and has been spotted.* Suffolk's *shadowing her and we're*

steaming to intercept. If everything goes according to plan we'll be in touch with her at dawn tomorrow. I don't have to say that I hope we'll make short work of her, with the help of Prince of Wales. *Let every man remember his duty. You'll be going to action stations soon after midnight—meanwhile I want the watch below to get all the rest they can. Now, in case I don't have another chance to speak to you: good luck to us all."*

The public-address system made itself heard in all parts of the ship, in the engine rooms and magazines, in the turrets and the wardroom, galleys and storerooms; and those final words, *Good luck to us all,* echoed in each compartment and were listened to by different groups of men—resigned, exalted, indifferent, nervous—every kind of reaction according to temperament.

From the darkened bridge of the *Prince of Wales* came a quick word.

"Signal from the flag, sir. Speed 27 knots."

"Very good. Call the captain. Ring down for 244 revolutions."

The officer stepped to the voice-pipe and spoke down to the operations room. *"Increasing speed to 27 knots."*

In the operations room, the voice-pipe came down through the deck overhead and terminated over the table on which the chart was spread. The navigating officer, bent over the chart, heard the words *Increasing speed to 27 knots* and repeated them back before making a note of time and position.

The captain and the captain's secretary came in at that moment.

"There's a long signal coming in from *Hood*, sir," said the secretary. "Here's the first page."

While the captain read it, another message dropped down the message tube, and another—the captain reading hastily as they were handed to him.

"Here's what we were waiting for," he said. "*Suffolk*'s

shadowing *Bismarck* in Denmark Strait, 65° North 28° West's where the admiral expects to make contact. Let's see."

"HERE, sir," said the navigating officer. He made a black cross on the chart, just like the black cross on *Hood*'s chart.

"Yes," said the captain. "I hope we're in a condition to fight."

On the mess deck of the *Prince of Wales*, there were strange figures mingled with the ratings there: workmen in civilian clothes, some in overalls, others more pretentious. Heralded by a pipe, the commander came in on his nightly rounds, looking keenly about him.

"You men comfortable all right?" he asked of one party of workmen.

"No, we're not," said one of the workmen, still seated. "We don't like sleeping in hammocks, and we don't like the food, and we don't like being taken away like this without our consent. What our union will say when we get home–"

"I expect you'll get double time and danger money," said the commander.

"'Tisn't the union I'm thinking about, sir," said another, less belligerent, "it's my wife. I can just guess what she thinks I'm up to."

"She'll be all the more pleased when she hears you haven't been," said the commander.

"Any idea when we're likely to get home, sir?"

"I haven't, and if I had I'm afraid I wouldn't tell you. Cheer up, men, we all have duties to do in wartime."

Another of the civilian workers was obviously thinking about something else.

"D'you feel that, sir?" he asked. "Listen! We're increasing speed. Feel that vibration? Must be 27 knots, I should think. May be 28. No, 27."

"You know these engines better than I do," said the commander.

"I helped to build 'em, and I've been helping to run 'em

for the last three days. I ought to know 'em. What are we putting on speed for, in the middle of the night like this?"

At this moment a breathless messenger came running up to the commander, saluted, and presented a note, which the commander studied. Then he dismissed the messenger.

"I may as well tell you now," he said. "It will be on the loud-speaker in a minute . . . . *Bismarck*'s been spotted. She's not far ahead of us, and we'll fight her in the morning."

"Fight her, sir? But those turbines—"

"You'll have to help keep 'em turning," said the commander.

The first speaker was on his feet, his grievances no longer apparent.

"We're going to fight, are we?" he said. "That shell ring in Y turret . . . I've never been satisfied with it, and I'm not satisfied with it now. I'd like to see what I can do. Can I go up there, sir?"

"I don't doubt you'll be welcome. Good luck with it."

In the background, two more civilian workers were exchanging comments.

"Look at this," said one of them. "Here it is in black and white: 'Henry J. Jones, noncombatant.' Same for you. Look—'noncombatant.'"

"That's to cover us if we're taking prisoner. Then they won't shoot us as spies. They'll put us into a civilian prison instead of a military one."

"But how can they take us prisoner?"

"If they pick us up after this ship's sunk. We might live long enough if the water's not too cold."

"But they can't fight with us on board! 'Tisn't legal."

"Ask the captain to put you ashore then," said the first speaker. "I'm going up to Y turret."

Any further words of his were drowned in the blare of the loud-speaker calling the men to action stations.

On the bridge of the *Bismarck* the admiral and captain were standing looking into the gray mist where the first light of dawn was beginning to show. The radio officer was reporting to them.

"The British cruiser has been sending out messages every fifteen minutes regularly all through the night, sir."

"Can you guess what they are?"

"I can be quite sure, sir. They are position and course reports."

"We could be sure of that in any case," said Lutjens to Lindemann. "What else?"

"I think I can identify her by her call sign, sir. She's the *Suffolk.*"

"Eight-inch-gun cruiser; 10,000 tons. Launched 1926. Last known captain, Ellis," said one of the staff, flipping through a reference book.

"Thank you, but the details hardly matter. Anything else?"

"The British Admiralty has been sending messages all through the night, sir. Some of them clearly address to ships—other ships besides the *Suffolk,* sir."

"No indication of which ships, or where?"

"I regret not, sir."

"Not a word from anything at sea?"

"Not a word, sir."

"Thank you."

As the radio officer saluted and turned away, Lutjens addressed Lindemann.

"That's radio silence enforced as it ought to be enforced. We could wish the British weren't so careful. But now we say good-by to Denmark Strait, and the Atlantic lies ahead of us. Tell me your opinion. Do you think there is anything to stop us?"

Lindemann hesitated to speak. He did not want to appear too optimistic.

"Tell me, Captain, please," persisted Lutjens.

"Unless the British moved instantly to the right place, without wasting an hour, the Atlantic should be open to us, sir."

"Then we'll give the *Suffolk* the slip, and there won't be

a convoy that dare move between America and England," said Lutjens triumphantly.

A telephone squawked beside them, and an officer sprang to it.

"Bridge," he said, and listened to the message before announcing it loudly. *"Smoke on the port bow!"*

As everyone else swung to look he continued to relay the messages.

"Ship on the port bow! Two ships on the port bow. Closing fast!"

A battery of binoculars was trained in that direction.

"Sound the alarm!" said Lutjens.

The bellowing warning brought the whole ship's company to their feet and to their stations.

"Two cruisers?" asked Lutjens.

"Big cruisers if that's what they are," answered Lindemann.

He and his admiral were each looking through binoculars and then taking their eyes away from them to address remarks to the other. Through the binoculars the gray shapes were steadily acquiring definition as the mist thinned.

"Signal *Eugen* to take station astern," snapped Lutjens. "Captain, open fire as soon as they are in range."

"They're coming right at us," said Lindemann. "They mean to fight."

"It might be better for 'em if they turned to give us their broadsides," answered Lutjens.

Telephones were squawking still.

"All turrets manned and ready!" announced the officer of the watch. *"Turrets training!"*

'They could see that from the bridge: the huge guns swinging round to point over the port bow.

"Remember what I said, Captain? We must be ready to blow any enemy out of the water at any minute, and here we are," said Lutjens, binoculars to his eyes.

"Those aren't cruisers," said Lindemann. "Look! They're coming round. That's the *Hood!* The *Hood!* And that's a battleship with her!"

His last words were cut off short by the roar of the first salvo from *Bismarck*'s guns.

"Hit her! Hit her! Keep on hitting her!" said Lutjens. The gunsmoke swirled round him.

In the operations room of the *Hood* the navigating officer was bent over his chart again, the one with the conspicuous black cross marked to the southward of Denmark Strait.

"There we are, sir. We ought to sight them during the next five minutes. We must be closing them fast."

"Not long to wait now," said the admiral.

"Guns loaded, sir," said another voice.

Down in a turret, the guns' crews were waiting beside the guns. Nobby was there, one of the guns' crews. They were standing ready.

"Can't be long now," said the man beside Nobby.

"Now we do our stuff," said Nobby. "Now it's our turn."

"Enemy in sight," said the officer commanding the turret. "Stand by!"

"Turret's training!" said Nobby, feeling the turret turn while the ship still heaved and rolled on the heavy sea.

The men exchanged glances. There were plenty of men among them who had not yet experienced action, who had never heard their guns fire at an enemy, who had never before waited—as they were waiting now—for an enemy's deadly shells to come winging over the waves to crash against—or through—the armor beside them. It was a nervous little interval, those few seconds when everything was ready, when drill had carried them through to this moment, without time to think until now. Thoughts could make prodigious leaps in a few seconds, back to memories of homes in England, forward to vague, almost unimaginable horrors.

"Wish we'd start," said somebody.

Somebody else was drumming with his fingers on the breech block in front of him.

"Keep your minds on your work," snapped the gun

captain.

Then the guns went off with a crash, and the long-practiced drill began, as the breeches swung open, the new shells came up—were rammed in—were followed by the charges, which were rammed in behind them—and the breeches slammed shut again.

"Right gun ready!"

"Left gun ready!"

Another salvo went off. The men bent to their work with frantic energy. A crash and a flash in the turret made them all stagger.

"They hit us!"

"Who cares?" said Nobby. "Come on!"

The next shells were rammed home as smoke came swirling into the turret.

The sea was boiling with splashes as the tall pillars of water rose up round the embattled ships. Funnel smoke and gunsmoke swirled over the heavy gray surface. The eye could travel across to the *Bismarck,* rolling deeply in the swell, and the imagination could penetrate through her armored side to the shellroom of the forward turrets. Here a small team of German sailors was at work, jerkily, putting the huge shells into the hoist, standing by for a moment, then sending them up and instantly addressing themselves to the next. A bearded German petty officer was standing to supervise; beside him was on e of the very young supernumerary officers. The petty officer was speaking, his speech punctuated by pauses as he checked the positioning of the shells in the hoist, and by the constant accompaniment of the thunder of the salvoes far overhead.

"This is *our* turn, sir, you see," he said. "Me and my men here. They can make all the plans they like in the Marineamt in Berlin. Admiral Raeder can look at his charts, and Admiral Lutjens up on the bridge can make his plans, and Captain Lindemann can issue his orders, but it's the guns that do the work. And if we down here don't keep the shells going up, the guns can't fire, and the admiral might as well be back at home. You see how it is, sir."

There was a brief pause as he corrected the placing of one of the shells.

"Up you go, my beauty," said the bearded petty officer. He blew a kiss to the shell as it vanished upward from sight up the hoist. It might perfectly well have been the very shell that had been sent aboard to the cry of "One more!" back in Gdynia harbor. Up the hoist it went; it slid onto the ring, swung round, rose up into the turret, was seized by the rammer and thrust into the breech of the gun with the turret's sweating crew grouped round. The charge followed it and then the guns went off with a crash. Lutjens on the bridge watching through his glasses said:

"That's a hit! Look! Look!"

An enormous pillar of smoke arose from the *Hood*.

Lindemann through his glasses saw it too. First there was the silhouette of the ship, sharp and clear now that she had emerged entirely from the mist. Then from somewhere just forward of the funnel came a jet of thick gray smoke. But before this had finished its course, before it had begun to mushroom out, a dozen other jets of smoke, each larger than the first, burst from the ship, expanding so that close above the ship they united, still soaring upwards and still expanding to form a dense cloud hanging over the ship from a great height, attached to it by a vague and slender stalk. It was in that moment that Lindemann, through his excellent binoculars, believed he could see great fragments of the ship soaring upwards to the cloud, outstripped by the jets at first but reaching the smoke now that it was nearly stationary. And he was nearly sure that he saw bow and stern of the ship rise up out of the water and the waist sink, as though a wanton child had seized a bathtub toy and snapped it across the middle.

It was only for that moment that Lindemann saw this. The broken-backed toy was instantly engulfed in further smoke, pouring from every aperture of the ship, lying low on the surface so that there was nothing to be seen except the few brief splashes as the high-tossed fragments of masts and decks and armor plate came arrowing back into the sea. And when this lower pall of smoke lifted and thinned there was nothing to be seen. Nothing.

And of Nobby and his friends in the turret there was nothing. One moment they had been hard at work, bending and heaving to the hard harsh light of the electric lamps; they were boxed up in their little room, separated from the world around them and above them by armor plate of steel a foot thick; below them the deep sea—below them the magazine and shellroom and three hundred tons of high explosive. For one moment it had been thus; the next, and the shell which *Bismarck* had sent hurtling towards them had crashed its way, as though endowed with malignant intelligence, through the chink in *Hood*'s armor, along the narrow unguarded route to the magazine below the turret, there to burst among those three hundred tons of high explosive. In that second, Nobby and his friends passed, without a chance of knowing it, from existence to annihilation.

In the War Room the tension was enormous. The rear admiral was still entertaining the air vice marshal.

"If *Hood*'s where we think she is they'll be making contact any moment," he said. "Daylight's just beginning in Denmark Strait now."

"Where's *Bismarck*?" asked the air vice marshal.

"By *Suffolk*'s last report ten minutes ago she was HERE."

The rear admiral pointed to the spot on the chart where the two courses marked in crayon intersected. He drew a black cross there.

"Signal from *Suffolk*, sir!" said the young officer at a voice-pipe at the table where the messages arrived. "Most immediate signal: HAVE SIGHTED *Hood* AND *Prince of Wales* BEARING SOUTHEAST, DISTANCE FIFTEEN MILES, COURSE SOUTHWEST."

"They've done it! They've got 'em."

There was excitement and exhilaration throughout the

War Room.

"Two minutes more and they'll sight the *Bismarck!*" said the rear admiral. "That's right."

The last words were called forth by a sight of the messages already spoken down the voice-pipe now delivered by pneumatic tube. The rear admiral hardly glanced at it.

"Most immediate signal from *Suffolk,*" announced the officer at the voice-pipe: *Hood* AND *Bismarck* OPENING FIRE. *Hood*'S COURSE APPROXIMATELY, SOUTHWEST."

"*Hood's* closing in on her," said the rear admiral. Once more he paid almost no attention to the written signal handed him.

"Most immediate signal from *Suffolk* coming through," said the young officer. He was clearly pretending not to be excited; he was making a show of iron calm. And in that moment all his calm disappeared. He seemed to wilt. "What's that? Repeat that." He sat at the voice-pipe doing nothing for a moment.

"Get on with your job, man," snapped the rear admiral.

The young officer turned a face of tragedy towards him.

"*Hood*'s blown up."

"What?"

At this moment the written message rattled down the tube. A dozen hands reached for it and the rear admiral tore it from the container.

"*Hood* BLOWN UP," he said. "*Hood* BLOWN UP."

"But what—what—" stammered the air vice marshal. The rear admiral had only a look for him. All round there were people standing as if turned to stone.

"*Hood!*" said an officer at length. "My brother Dick—"

An elderly commander, most polite up to that moment, collided with the WREN officer beside the chart.

"Get out of my way, damn you," he snapped, and then, his tone softened. "The *Hood*'s sunk! The *Hood*'s sunk!"

The rear admiral rallied.

"Go back to your duties," he snapped. "We've more to

do."

Another message was being spoken down the voice-pipe, and the young officer braced himself to hear.

"Most immediate signal from *Suffolk*," he announced, in a curious parody of his earlier tone: "*Hood* SUNK. *Prince of Wales* AND *Bismarck* EXCHANGING FIRE."

"Perhaps *Prince of Wales*'ll do her business for her," said the air vice marshal to an unresponsive audience.

The written message this time received careful attention.

"Most immediate message *Suffolk*," announced the young officer: "*Prince of Wales* HEAVILY HIT. *Prince of Wales* ON FIRE FORWARD. *Prince of Wales* WITHDRAWING FROM ACTION BEHIND SMOKE SCREEN."

"*Prince of Wales* beaten," said the rear admiral in a voice devoid of expression. When the message was given him he stood holding it without a glance. Another officer at the table intervened at this moment.

"Wireless interception speaking, sir. Powerful signals in

German code, originating in Denmark Strait. *Bismarck* calling Berlin, sir."

"They'll be telling the world," said the rear admiral. "Oh, God! They'll be telling the world."

All through the *Prince of Wales*—in the engine room where the turbines sang their high-pitched song, in the magazine, in the wardroom, laid out as a hospital, in the turrets—the ship's loud-speaker began an announcement, heralded by a pipe.

"Men of the Prince of Wales! *The captain has ordered me to let you in on what's going on out here. Captain's secretary speaking from the bridge. Enemy's in sight and we're closing in on her. There's* Hood *firing now. Our turn in a moment."*

The broadcast was interrupted by the bellow of the guns heard through the loud-speaker. Down in the engine room the civilian workman was saying, "Watch that collar there. It'll run hot if you give it half a chance."

Up in Y turret, another civilian saw the guns recoil, the

fresh shells and charges come up, and the rammers flash into action and disappear again.

"All right that time," he said. "I'll get down and look at that shell ring."

Two decks down was the shell ring with shells rising on the hoist and positioning themselves upon it. The loud-speaker was still announcing:

"*Splashes all round the* Bismarck. *We're doing well. The* Hood—" The voice stopped for several seconds, and when it resumed it was in a broken tone. "*The* Hood—*the* Hood—"

The loud-speaker stopped with a click.

"What's happened to the *Hood?*" asked one of the ratings by the shell ring.

"You just watch that switch there and don't worry about anything else," said the civilian.

"*Men of the* Prince of Wales," began the loud-speaker again. *The captain's told me to tell you. The* Hood*'s gone. Blown up and sunk. A brave ship and now we've seen the* *last of her. Now it's up to us. We've got* Bismarck's *measure and we'll see it through.*"

"*Hood* gone? All those chaps?" said someone by the shell ring.

On the bridge of the *Prince of Wales* the captain and officers were looking out through a forest of splashes. The captain's secretary at the loud-speaker was saying, "Now it's up to us. We've got . . . " and so on.

Down the voice-pipe the officer of the watch was saying, *Course* 240°." In the operations room just below, the officer at the chart table heard the words through the tube and repeated them, bending over the chart.

Down by the shell ring the loud-speaker began again.

"*Captain says you're doing well, me. Keep on . . .* "

The words ended in a frightful crash heard deafeningly over the loud-speaker.

"They've copped it up there," said a voice at the shell ring.

The whole bridge was a mass of flaming wreckage and heaped corpses. In the chartroom below, the navigating officer saw something drip out of the voice-pipe onto the chart before him.

"What on earth? He put his hand out and touched it. "My God, it's blood!" It went on dropping thickly down upon the chart.

Upon the bridge a tattered, smoke-blackened figure crawled to the voice-pipe and pulled aside the corpse which lay across the mouth.

"Hard a-port. Steer one-five-o. Hard a-port."

Hard a-port," repeated the navigating officer in the chartroom. The ship heeled violently as the helm went over, so that the navigating officer had to hold on to save himself.

Far in the depths of the turret down in the traverser space the heel was felt and the men had to hold on. There was a clatter and crash and the ring slipped from its rollers and crashed over lopsided. A shell slid off and trapped the civilian worker there by the leg with its three-quarters-of-a-ton weight. He cried out with pain. As the shell ring crew turned to help him he forced himself to speak normally.

"All right, chums. Tell 'em up above the ring's jammed. Y turret won't fire until you've cleared it." The shell moved a little on his leg.

"A-ah," he said in agony, and fainted.

On the bridge of the *Bismarck* Lutjens and Lindemann were looking through their binoculars with the guns bellowing below them. On the horizon lay the pall of smoke which marked the end of the *Hood*. Not far from it was the silhouette of the *Prince of Wales*, almost masked with smoke and shell splashes.

"Battleship's turning away," said Lutjens. "More smoke. Yes, she's making smoke. She's running!"

The guns fell suddenly silent and a staff officer at a telephone reported formally. "Range obscured."

Simultaneously Lutjens and Lindemann took their glasses from their eyes and faced each other.

"This is victory, sir," said Lindemann. "A crushing, decisive victory for which your name will always be remembered. It is my proud privilege to be the first to congratulate you."

They shook hands; the rest of the staff were standing by with exultation on their faces.

"Thank you, Captain," said Lutjens. Even while his right hand was still being clasped he was gesturing to his chief of staff with his left.

"Send this news to Berlin at once," he said. "See that it gets off instantly."

"Aye aye, sir."

In the broadcasting station in Berlin an announcer, script in hand, stood at the microphone. At a gesture from the controller behind the window a trumpeter put his instrument to his lips and blew a long triumphant fanfare.

"Citizens of the Reich!" began the announcer. "We interrupt our program to bring you marvelous news. Our ships in the Atlantic have won a great, a marvelous victory. Our Reich Navy is triumphant at sea. The proud British battle-cruiser *Hood* has been blown to atoms, has been sunk with all hands under the guns of our naval forces. The rest of the British Navy has turned and fled, hiding themselves behind a smoke screen from the vengeance of the Reich. Another British battleship has been hit over and over again, and by this time she has probably gone down to join the *Hood* in the icy waters of Denmark Strait. Ten thousand British sailors have paid the price of obedience to the warmongering Churchill and his Jewish clique. Let us all join in heartfelt congratulations to our Führer, who made this possible. One people, one State, one Führer!"

All over Germany the news was broadcast. It was heard with exultation in houses and in factories, in hospitals and in cafés.

In the British Ministry of Information telephones were ringing.

"Berlin's got the news on the air already. Hurry up with that announcement. Better to hear it from us than from them. Hurry up with it."

"Not easy to write a bulletin about defeat," answered the telephone.

"Give the facts, man. They've got to hear about it, and they can take it."

In the factories light music coming over the wireless ended abruptly and a calm B.B.C. voice made itself heard:

"The Admiralty regrets to announce the loss with all hands of H.M.S. *Hood* this morning as a result of enemy action in Denmark Strait. Further action is imminent."

In the bombed-out streets of Portsmouth an elderly mother was walking with her shopping bag. She stopped when she saw a newspaper seller beginning to write up a headline on his contents bill.

"H-O-O-D," he began, and then went on "S-U-N-K." The woman stood staring and horrified for some seconds, the tears beginning to run down her cheeks. She turned away, bowed with sorrow.

"You all right, Ma?" asked a special policeman.

She straightened up with her cheeks still wet.

"Yes, I'm all right."

She had not far to go with her shopping bag; round the corner where the heap of rubble marked where two houses had once stood, along to her little house with the boards replacing its shattered windows. She entered and put down her bag. There was a framed photograph on the table, of someone in a seaman's uniform, and she sat down where she could see it, dark though the room was with its boarded-up windows.

"I said I was all right," she said aloud to herself.

Her old woman's face was disfiguring itself, was growing shapeless with the emotions within her. Her wizened form seemed to shrink still further as she folded down upon herself.

"Oh, Nobby, Nobby," she said, and now her face was down upon her skinny knees and her narrow back shook with her sobs.

The New York newspapers carried vast headlines. *Bismarck* SINKS *Hood*. WORLD'S BIGGEST BATTLE CRUISER BLOWN UP . . . . And in a New York building a news commentator was explaining to his audience what had happened.

"The news has already reached you by our instant service, and at the moment there is no further bulletin at hand. It's quite obvious that the *Bismarck* was on her way to break out into the Atlantic, and the British tried to stop her. And it's also obvious that the British have suffered a stunning defeat. The *Hood* has blown up. That means the loss of an important ship and a great many lives. The dead will number a thousand at least, perhaps two thousand. Two thousand men killed in a single moment. And that's not all. The German bulletin goes on to say that another British battleship was badly damaged, possibly sunk. There's no reason to doubt the truth of this. The British have suffered a very serious disaster. And the question is, what happens next? The *Bismarck* has complete freedom of action—the British make no claim to having damaged her in the least. What will she do? We can be sure that there is no British ship within hundreds of miles of her who can fight her. She can come south into the Atlantic and smash the British convoys—no convoy escort could stand up to her for a moment. There are probably German tankers waiting for her at a secret rendezvous—she may go raging round the Atlantic for months disrupting British commerce. You must remember, besides, that there are also in Brest two German battlecruisers, the *Scharnhorst* and the *Gneisenau*. The British have to watch them all the time in case they break out too, which means they have to fight the *Bismarck* with one hand tied behind them. What are the chances of catching her? My information is that now that the *Hood*'s gone there is no British battleship to compare with her in any way for speed or size or fighting power. The damage she may do is quite incalculable, even if she might be caught at last—and she may never be. And there's something else she can do, too. She can turn round and return to Germany, round Iceland either to the east or to the west. If she turns up at home safe and sound after a victory as tremendous as this, Dr. Goebbels will be able to make a fine story out of it, especially as there appears no reason why she should not come out at any time and repeat the exploit. I've been a good friend to the British, as you know, but this time they seem to be really up against it. It's not only in the Atlantic that they're having their troubles, but over in the Mediterranean, in Greece and in Crete and in North Africa . . . "

Lindemann and Lutjens were looking at the chart in the *Bismarck*.

"We could go back, sir," said Lindemann. "They'd never intercept us."

"Why should we?"

"We've won a great victory, and if the German radio could announce that we were back again unscathed the world would—"

"The world would know at least that we had won a victory and had not wanted to gather the fruits of it. Risks are meant to be taken in war, Captain. Think of the possibilities before us in the Atlantic. Are we going to turn back and waste them? Remember what I did with the *Scharnhorst* and *Gneisenau*. Propaganda's all very well, but even Dr. Goebbels himself would admit that wars are won by deeds, not words."

"But the British—"

"I doubt if the British can lift a finger against us for days to come. Forward! We'll shake that British cruiser off and then we'll be free. Think of those convoys, Captain."

"I shall think about them, sir. Well, Commander?"

The executive officer had arrived and had saluted, waiting to make a report.

"We were hit by one shell, Captain. At Number 46 station, port side."

"Where's that?" demanded the admiral.

"Forward, sir. It's over Number 2 oil fuel tank. With the tank full I cannot yet investigate the damage, except that I can say for certain that it's only slight, very slight indeed."

"And that's all the damage?" asked the admiral.

"Yes, sir. But the fuel tank is leaking oil. If you would come this way, sir—" He led the way to the port wing of the bridge, and they looked over at the water boiling along beside the ship.

"You see, sir? We're leaving a little oil behind us. The tank is being pumped out and the fuel transferred at this moment, sir."

"Then we need not give it another thought," said the admiral.

"No, sir," said the commander, and hesitated. "Except—except that the fuel has been contaminated with sea water. We had two hundred tons less fuel than we thought we had."

"I understand," said the admiral.

"There's still plenty of time to go back, sir," suggested Lindemann.

"I understand that, too," said the admiral. "Thank you, Commander."

Lutjens and Lindemann stood staring at the map.

"Two hundred tons less oil," said Lindemann—"and that's a permanent loss, sir, while we stay at sea. When we meet our tankers it will be two hundred tons less that we shall be able to take on board."

"Yes," said Lutjens, still thinking deeply. His forefinger was sweeping out arcs on the chart. He talked more to himself than to Lindemann. "The decision I have to take—the next words I say—can change the history of the world, can decide the fate of nations, can settle the destiny of Germany and of National Socialism and of our Führer. Ten thousand—twenty thousand—fifty thousand lives can be cut short by my next order."

"That is so, sir."

"Forward—back. This is the last moment in which to

choose. No changing of minds after this."

"I've given you my opinion, sir."

"No!" said Lutjens suddenly. "I shall go forward. We haven't fought our way out into the Atlantic just to go back again tamely. Forward! We shall have to turn aside into Brest. Two days there and the damage can be repaired. Then, with the *Scharnhorst* and the *Gneisenau,* I shall sail out again at the head of a squadron incomparable for power and speed."

"Very well, sir."

"And there are British convoys which may be across our path. Our U-boats can guide us to them. Forward!"

"Very well, sir. Will you give me my definitive orders?"

"Maintain our present course for today until we've shaken off that cruiser. Then we can shape a course for Brest. I don't think the British will guess what we intend."

"Very well, sir."

In the War Room at the Admiralty a group of officers, including the admiral, the rear admiral and the air vice marshal, were standing by the chart.

"Signal from *Suffolk,* sir," said a young officer, reading aloud. "*Bismarck* STILL HEADING SOUTHWEST, SPEED 25 KNOTS. *Bismarck* LOSING OIL AND LEAVING A BROAD TRAIL OF OIL BEHIND HER."

"She was hit, then!" said the rear admiral.

"She's still doing 25 knots all the same," said the admiral. "Some small leak in an oil fuel tank . . . What's the last weather report?"

"Foul as usual," said the air vice marshal. "Cloud at 1000 feet, heavy banks of fog, wind force 5, heavy swell."

"Every chance of the *Suffolk* losing her, then. Can your fellows help?"

"As far as we can, sir. She's getting pretty far from Iceland, I'm afraid."

An officer approached the chart to change the position of the Home Fleet on it.

"Tovey's THERE," said the admiral. "If *Bismarck* holds her present course he'll make contact tomorrow. What's the figure for that?"

"Twelve noon, sir," answered an officer at a plotting board.

"IF*Bismarck* holds her course . . . Every ship we have must move to cut her off. There's *Rodney*. Let her leave her convoy and take up a course to intercept. *Ramillies*—she can leave her convoy, too. Cable to Halifax and have *Revenge* leave as soon as she can get up steam. Call in *London* and *Edinburgh* from their convoys and send them north as well. Now, Force H. What about Somerville?"

"He's at sea, sir."

"Right. Let me see how that will look at this time tomorrow."

"Yes, sir. I can do it now."

On another table lay another chart of the North Atlantic, and an officer began to draw lines upon it: for the *Bis-*

marck's course; for the Home Fleet and Force H; for *Ramillies* and *Rodney* and *Revenge;* for the cruisers . . .

"Here's *Bismarck* and *Suffolk* at noon tomorrow if she holds her course."

"IF," said the admiral.

"Home Fleet," said the officer. "Force H . . . Cruisers . . . *Ramillies* . . . *Rodney* . . . *Revenge* . . . *London* . . . *Edinburgh* . . . "

The line of the *Bismarck* met the line of the Home Fleet. At the same time from every direction converged the other black lines towards that point, some coming close, some ending far away, but all together making upon the mind a most powerful impression of overwhelming force.

"It looks well enough on paper," said the admiral. Draft the orders at once."

"The Prime Minister, sir," said another officer, hurrying into the room.

"I'll come," said the admiral. "Let's have that with me."

He strode across into a side room and someone laid the

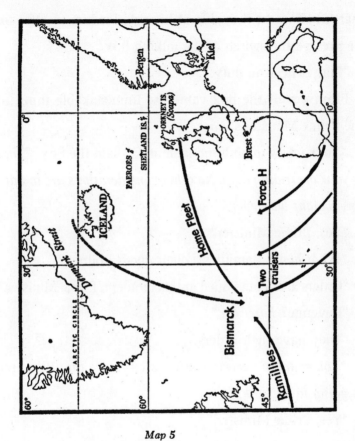

Map 5

"It looks well enough on paper."

marked chart on the table at his side for him to refer to. He pressed the switch of the talking box.

"Flag officer on duty."

From out of the box came the unmistakable tones of the Prime Minister's voice."

"Your job is to sink the Bismarck," said the box. *"That is your overriding duty. No other considerations are to have any weight whatever."*

"Yes, Prime Minister."

"What about Ramillies? *What about* Rodney?"

"Orders are being issued at this moment, Prime Minister."

"Revenge? *Force H?"*

"They have their orders."

"You're taking every possible step to see that Bismarck *is going to be sunk?"*

"Yes, Prime Minister."

"Not only the possible steps, not only the easy steps and the obvious steps, but the difficult steps and the almost impossible steps, and all the quite impossible steps you

can manage as well. The eyes of the whole world are upon us."

"You don't have to remind me about that, Prime Minister."

"Well, remember. Sink the Bismarck. *Good-by."*

"Most immediate signal from *Suffolk,* sir," said the young officer. "She's under fire from *Bismarck."*

In the *Suffolk* the scene was very similar to the earlier one before the tragedy of the *Hood.* She was still steaming hard over the misty water, sliding out of one fogbank for a few brief minutes before sliding into another. The lookouts were still at their stations, the exposed ones still pelted with spray, still turning steadily with their binoculars as they swept the sea all around the ship.

"Ship bearing green 5!" yelled one of the forward lookouts suddenly. There was the *Bismarck,* bows on, heading out of the mist straight for her.

Down the voice-pipe above the head of the quartermaster at the wheel came the sharp order:

"Hard a-port."

Instantly the quartermaster swung the wheel round, feeling the heel of the ship as she turned, watching the compass move steadily over the card.

Down in the boiler room the telegraphs rang for full speed, and a clattering indicator said MAKE SMOKE. The maneuvering valves were feverishly turned, as the ship heeled. A stoker opened the valve to make smoke, and, peering through the peephole, saw the white-hot flames roaring behind it become thick and black.

On the bridge Dusty at his post saw the horizon swinging round in his binoculars as he had to steady himself against the heel of the ship, and then as she straightened on the new course he saw *Bismarck* plain and clear. He saw the flames and smoke of the salvo she fired.

"Here it comes, mates," he said. The splashes from the salvo rose up a quarter of a mile from the ship's starboard quarter.

"Missed us that time," he said.

"Where's that smoke?" demanded a rating at the AA gun beside him. He looked up: a couple of preliminary puffs and then the smoke came eddying out, thick, black, and oily, pouring from the funnels and spreading in a dense pall behind them on the surface of the sea. Yet out of the very smoke, close alongside, rose the next columns of water as the second salvo hardly missed them. The water came tumbling on board to deluge the men near at hand. Dusty spluttered, wiping the water from his eyes and from his binoculars, and as he did so he heard the next salvo tear past overhead with a rumble like a train in a tunnel. He shook his fist at the *Bismarck,* invisible through the smoke.

On the bridge of the *Bismarck,* Lindemann and Lutjens were looking at the thick black pall of smoke lying on the surface of the sea.

"Can't risk going into that," said Lutjens. "Resume our

former course, if you please, Captain."

"Aye aye, sir."

He gave the order.

"Now make our last signal to *Eugen*," said Lutjens. "Good-by and good luck."

Far off on the horizon, almost invisible in the mist, a searchlight winked at them. The signal rating on the wing of the bridge read it off as the message came in.

"THANK YOU. GOOD-BY. BEST OF . . . Signal obscured in mist, sir."

"Thank you. We can guess the end," said Lutjens, and then, turning to Lindemann, "I wonder if we can?"

"At any rate *Eugen*'s got away unseen, sir. She'll have a clear run for home."

The chief of staff approached with a signal form in his hand and saluted.

"Signal just come through from the Marineamt in Berlin, sir," he said. "Our agent in Algeciras reports that Force H, carrier *Ark Royal,* battle cruiser *Renown,* cruiser *Sheffield,* and six destroyers left Gibraltar at midnight, heading west out of the Mediterranean."

"Very well. Let's come and see," said Lutjens.

They went into the chartroom, where a navigating officer was plotting hypothetical courses.

"Assuming we make our turn at midnight, that's our course, sir," he said. "Here's the best possible course for Force H."

"Do they intercept?"

"Hardly, sir."

"There'll be U-boats looking out for Force H. What's the weather report for that area?"

"Wind force 6 south to southwest, sir," said the chief of staff, running through a pad of messages. "Visibility poor, cloud ceiling 500 feet, heavy sea."

"I think we can discount Force H, then," said Lutjens. "That sea will slow down her screen, and she won't be able to get her planes into the air in any case."

"*Ark Royal*'s a very experienced ship, sir," said Lindemann.

"She can't read our minds, though," said Lutjens. "*Ark Royal* or no *Ark Royal*."

"The British have done pretty well along that line so far, sir," said Lindemann.

"How do you mean?"

"I'm referring to what happened today, sir, and all that it implies."

"Please be more specific."

"We left Norway in thick weather, sir. We took the best course for Denmark Strait, at our best speed. That was only one out of a dozen possible things we could have done. The British could only intercept us here, sir, by moving instantly, without wasting a moment."

"Well?"

"And they did, sir. At dawn this morning there were two ships cutting us off. You must agree, sir, that was remarkably intelligent anticipation."

"You forget, Captain, that it was just as likely to be remarkable good luck. In war, Captain, there is always the danger of attributing to the enemy uncanny powers and overwhelming strength . . . Until you meet him. As a result of their luck or their judgment, the British have suffered a stunning defeat. Let's hope the *Ark Royal* has the same sort of luck."

It was a lively evening in Gibraltar, as Force H was in and leave had been given to one watch. The bars were full of sailors drinking beer, the streets full of sailors wandering aimlessly. The cinema was full of sailors shouting with laughter at what was going on on the screen. When the picture suddenly came to a halt and the sound to an abrupt end, they attributed it to a mechanical failure and burst into catcalls, which died away into silence as a badly spelled and badly written announcement appeared, cast on the screen from a slide: "All naval personnel report on board at once." The announcement was greeted by a boo or two and a groan or two, but when the lights were turned on it could be seen that every man was on his feet and pushing for the doors. The patrols were going along the street.

"Get back to your ships. Leave canceled."

They went into the bars and interrupted the drinking, hustling the men out without ceremony. All about the Rock, sailors were hastening to their ships, leaning out of gharris to cheer on the drivers, running sweating along the roads, piling good-naturedly into boats. The *Ark Royal* was lying alongside and a steady river of men was pouring up the gangway into her. Oil fuel was being pumped into her from a tanker; miscellaneous stores were being hurried on board. Alongside her was a lighter, and the ship's crane was swinging torpedoes up into the ship.

"How many more of these things?" hailed an officer above.

"One more!" shouted the dockyard charge hand down in the lighter, waving a finger.

The crane took hold of the thing, swaying it ponderously

up from the lighter, up above the flight deck, and then down, down, through the hangar deck, where a working party took charge of it to place it in the torpedo stowage.

"That's the last of these beauties," said Ginger, the torpedo gunner's mate in charge. "One more for Mussolini!"

He slapped the thing on its flank; it seemed as malignant, as coldly menacing, as a fifteen-inch shell. Orders were already roaring through the ship for men to take their stations to prepare for sea. Signal lights were winking here and there in the bay. On the bridge a signal rating reported:

"Destroyers under way, sir."

"Very good."

The orders were given quietly for getting under way.

"Cast off for'ard. Cast off aft. Slow ahead port engines. Stop all engines. Wheel amidships. Stop all engines. Slow ahead all engines. Wheel amidships. Stop all engines. Slow ahead all engines. Half-speed all engines. Starboard fifteen."

Preceded by the destroyers, Force H was heading out

through the harbor defenses. The lights of La Linea and Algeciras circled on the horizon as the ship turned. On the catwalk two dark figures of Fleet Air Arm officers watched them circle.

"Every Nazi agent in Algeciras and La Linea and Ceua has his glasses trained on us at this moment," said one of them.

"And look," said the other. "They'll have something to say about it this time. See how we're turning?"

"We're going out!" said the other. "Not up the Mediterranean at all!"

Down in the torpedo stowage a rating arrived from up above to join Ginger's working party.

"We're saying good-by to the sunny Mediterranean," he announced. "Out into the broad Atlantic for us, boys."

"No!" exclaimed someone else.

"Yes. We're going through the Straits this minute."

"Maybe we're going home," said someone hopefully.

"Maybe we'll get some leave," added another more

hopefully still.

"Maybe we're going to get some work done," said Ginger, recalling them to their duties. He addressed the torpedo. "Come on you pig. You're not going to tickle Mussolini's ribs this time. Hitler for you, and the German Navy."

"Where d'you think we're going, P.O?"

"My friend Winston's forgotten to give me a ring. You'll have to wait until he does before we find out."

"Coo! Feel that!" said a rating.

Ark Royal was meeting the first of the Atlantic swell, and raising her bows high into the air, with everything not fastened down slipping and sliding and swinging, to hang poised and then plunge sideways as she corkscrewed over the sea. The destroyer screen was suffering more acutely, heaving and plunging over the confused waves as it felt its way into the Atlantic ahead of *Ark Royal* and *Renown*.

As to *Bismarck,* that ship was heaving and plunging similarly over a rough sea. Admiral Lutjens came out of his day cabin and walked to the bridge. He had three or four small leather cases in his hand.

"I wish to address the ship's company, Captain, and please parade the supernumerary officers."

At a sign from Lindemann, a petty officer switched on the public address system and called the crew's attention to the fact that the admiral was going to speak. The supernumerary officers were already parading on the afterdeck. Now they looked weary and battered, not having been to bed for several nights.

"Kindly send for Commander Schwartz and Lieutenant Commander Dollman," said Lutjens.

"Aye aye, sir," said Lindemann as the admiral approached the loud speaker.

"Men of the *Bismarck!* I cannot call you from your duties while a vigilant enemy lurks over the horizon. But while you are at your stations, tending your engines and manning your guns, you can hear what I have to say, while our young officers can witness the ceremonial. Men of the *Bismarck!* First I have to tell you of the great honor done us. Our Führer has sent me a personal message to convey to you, to Captain Lindemann and to every single man of the ship's company. Our Führer himself sends his congratulations to us all. He says—these are his very words—the news of our great victory will rock every capital in the world—the warmonger Churchill totters on his throne. He bids us go on and on, from victory to victory, until Jewry is utterly overthrown and the world can know peace again under our swastika banner of National Socialism."

The ship's political officer had been awaiting his cue, and stepped forward in front of the supernumerary officers with a gesture.

"Heil Hitler!" they piped, obediently. *"Sieg Heil! Sieg Heil!"*

It was not a very impressive exhibition; the boys were weary and perhaps halfhearted.

"The Führer's message went on to command me in his name—in the name of the Führer—to make awards to officers and men in this ship who have distinguished themselves. Lieutenant Commander Dollman!"

He came sheepishly forward.

"In the name of the Führer, I present you, the assistant gunnery officer of the *Bismarck*, with the Knight's Cross of the Iron Cross."

At a further gesture from the political officer the young officers cheered as Lutjens put the cross on Dollman.

"Commander Schwartz! As the gunnery officer of this ship you have played a principal part in the destruction of the *Hood*. In the name of the Führer, I present you with the Knight's Cross with Swords."

Again the young officers cheered.

"Your captain already proudly wears the Knight's Cross. Now, Captain Lindemann, it is my honor and pleasure to present you with the Knight's Cross with Swords and Diamonds!"

Lindemann was about to come forward to receive it when the general alarm blared through the ship.

"Air warning! Air warning! Enemy planes in sight! Planes on the port quarter!"

The AA guns were already training round; they had begun their fire before Lutjens and Lindemann had reached their posts on the bridge again. Here came nine Swordfish, coming in intolerably slowly, wheeling to get on the *Bismarck*'s bow and to drop their torpedoes from a good position.

"Hard a-starboard!" roared Lindemann.

The sky was pockmarked with the black puffs of smoke from the AA shells. The *Bismarck*s glittering wake nearly completed a circle as she turned, heeling violently.

"Hard a-port!" roared Lindemann, and the ship leaned over the other way as the helm was put over. Torpedoes streaked close by her sides, their wakes visible in the gray water. There was a roar and fountain of water as one torpedo exploded against her starboard bow. Then the attack was over as quickly as it was begun.

"Those were Swordfish," said Lutjens to his chief of staff. "How many did you count?"

"Seven, sir."

"And you?"

"I thought I saw nine."

"I thought there were nine as well."

"Swordfish means a carrier's within range, sir," said the chief of staff.

"Not a very well-equipped carrier, if all they can send into the attack is nine Swordfish," said Lutjens. "They scored a hit, all the same, up there on the starboard bow. What's the damage, Captain?"

"Report's just coming through, sir . . . ." Lindemann was listening on the telephone and nodding as he answered. "Very well . . . . Damage Control reports the injury done to the ship is negligible, sir. No one hurt. The pumps are already gaining on the water as it comes in. They'll have the hole patched in less than an hour. The ship's fighting aiblity is not impaired in the slightest, sir."

"Our *Bismarck* hardly has to give a thought to the little torpedoes a Swordfish can carry," said Lutjens. "Now let's see where they've come from."

He led the way into the chartroom and bent over the chart.

"What's the extreme range of a Swordfish?"

"M'm. Hundred and twenty miles. Less than a hundred and fifty anyway."

At a sign from Lutjens the navigating officer swept the compasses round in a circle.

"Somewhere inside there," said Lutjens. "A large area, gentlemen."

A young wireless officer made his appearance in the chartroom.

"Lieutenant Holder sent me, sir. We are taking in the wireless signals from the Swordfish."

"Yes?"

"By direction finding their course is a little north of

east—85°, sir, very approximately."

A glance at the navigating officer caused him to draw a line on that bearing from the ship's position to the circumference of the circle.

"A carrier. There," said Lutjens.

"And *Ark Royal*'s a thousand miles away," said the chief of staff with a gestsure at the other edge of the chart.

"A carrier with nine little Swordfish and no more . . . " said Lutjens. "When's sunset?"

"Seventeen minutes from now, sir," said the navigating officer.

"An hour for them to refuel and rearm . . . An hour to return here . . . No moon, and low cloud . . . They won't find us again tonight, sir," said the chief of staff.

"Nor tomorrow if we throw off that cruiser," said Lutjens. "As we will."

He went to clap one first into the other and discovered that he was still holding the leather case of the Iron Cross which he had intended to present to Lindemann.

"I'm forgetting one of my duties. Captain, in the Führer's name I make this presentation to you."

"Thank you, Admiral," said Lindemann.

"Long may you wear this badge of such great distinction."

"I hope I do, sir," said Lindemann, looking down at the glittering thing.

"We're entering into fog again, sir," said the chief of staff. "Now's our time."

In the War Room the admiral and the rear admiral and the air vice marshal, with others, were looking at the chart whereon were indicated the ships involved in the pursuit of the *Bismarck.*

"They're closing in on her all right," said the air vice marshal.

"Yes. It looks like it," said the admiral.

"Position, course and speed from *Suffolk,* sir," said a young officer. "*Bismarck*'s holding her course as before."

"I wonder what he has in mind?" said the admiral almost to himself. "The Home Fleet will be up to him by tomorrow noon."

"He doesn't know the Home Fleet's at sea, sir," said the rear admiral.

"Most immediate message from *Suffolk,* sir," said the young officer loudly: "HAVE SIGHTED NINE SWORDFISH PRO-CEEDING TOWARD *Bismarck.*"

"Nine Swordfish!" said the admiral. "That's *Victorious!* That's all she carried."

"If the Home Fleet's where we think it is, *Victorious* is nearly one hundred and fifty miles from *Bismarck,*" said someone doing some rapid work with dividers.

"Isn't there another report yet?" demanded the admiral.

"*Suffolk* reporting: HEAVY FIRING FROM *Bismarck.*"

"They're going into the attack," said the air vice marshal. "Why are there only nine of them?"

"*Victorious* is like the *Prince of Wales,*" said the rear

admiral. "She's brand-new from the builder's hands. Those Swordfish pilots have never risen from a carrier's deck before and never landed on again, either. They're raw. But that was all we had when *Bismarck* came out."

"*Suffolk* reporting," said the young officer: "Firing ceased from *Bismarck.*"

"Attack's over one way or the other then," said the air vice marshal.

"*Suffolk* reporting: HAVE INTERCEPTED SIGNAL FROM AIRCRAFT TO *Victorious*. ONE HIT OBSERVED."

"Please God that'll slow her up," said the rear admiral. "That's what Tovey sent them off to do."

"My guess is she could take half a dozen or more without too much damage," said the admiral.

"*Suffolk* reporting position, course and speed," said the young officer.

"What's the course and speed?" demanded the rear admiral.

"Course 190°, speed 25 knots."

"No change in either. Doesn't look as if that hit's had any effect," said the admiral.

"It's just sunset over there," said the rear admiral. "Dark before long. Foggy, too."

"And the wind's freshening all the time. Those Swordfish pilots will be flying on for the first time in their lives with a huge sea running, in the dark and the fog. Please God they make it," said the admiral.

"*Suffolk* reporting," said the young officer: "HAVE LOST CONTACT WITH *Bismark*. AM MAKING SEARCH."

"Lost her?" said the admiral.

"Darkness and fog," said the rear admiral. "Can't believe she'll find her again."

The radio commentator in New York was standing by his mike again.

"Well," he said. "It's now just twenty-four hours after I told you about the *Bismarck* sinking the *Hood*. Since that first announcement there hasn't been a single word from the British government. It's just as if the *Bismarck* didn't exist as far as John Bull is concerned. But we've been hearing plenty from Dr. Goebbles and the Nazi government. Berlin says that yesterday evening the British attacked *Bismarck* with aircraft from a carrier, and they go on to say—I'm telling you what Berlin says—that the attack was beaten off with no damage to *Bismarck* and heavy loss to the attackers. It may well be true. I'd like to point out that if this attack *did* take place, it's the first time in the history of the world that planes have taken off from a carrier to attack a German battleship at sea. German battleships in harbor and Italian battleships have been attacked—remember what the British did at Taranto. But this is the first time that planes from a carrier have attacked a German battleship at sea. Moreover, that battleship is modern and well manned and full of fight, as we saw yesterday. I expect that attack was made, and, reluctant though I am to believe all that Dr. Goebbels said, I expect that attack failed. Otherwise by now we'd be hearing something from London. And the significance of it is that the *Bismarck* is out on the rampage. That Swordfish attack was a desperate attempt to slow her up. It did not do so. Will the English ever be able to catch her now? Finding one ship in the Atlantic is like finding one particular automobile in the State of Texas. And if that automobile is bigger and faster and more powerful than anything you have to chase it with—well, you can see how it is. If ever things looked gloomy for Britain, it's today. There's Crete, you know . . . "

All over the world the question was being asked: "Where is the *Bismarck?*" In a thousand newspapers in a hundred languages that question appeared as a front-page headline.

And the *Bismarck* was actually laboring at her best speed across the stormy Atlantic towards St. Nazaire. There was half a gale still blowing, as ever, and the sea was wild. This was her fourth successive day at sea without any relaxation for her crew save what small comfort they could derive from lying on the steel decks close to their action stations. Beards were sprouting everywhere, even on the cheeks of the young supernumerary officers. Lutjens was in his armchair overcome by the need for sleep when his chief of staff entered.

"News about Scapa Flow at last, sir," he said. "The Luftwaffe were able to reconnoiter this morning."

"And what did they see?"

"Nothing, sir. Not a battleship or a carrier or a cruiser there. The British Home Fleet's at sea, sir, somewhere. And it may have been at sea for a long time, for it was three days ago that the last reconnaissance of Scapa Flow was made."

"I think we could know the British were at sea by now without the Luftwaffe to tell us," said Lutjens.

"Yes, sir."

"Oh, I suppose we'd better look at the chart again."

Lindemann joined them as they bent over it.

"In three days the Home Fleet could have reached pretty nearly anywhere in the Eastern Atlantic," said Lutjens.

"Oh yes, sir," said the chief of staff, a little condescendingly. "At 20 knots—" He made a wide sweep of the compasses over the chart—"they could be anywhere inside THERE, sir."

"Yes," said Lutjens, tapping the chart at the cross which marked *Bismarck's* position. It lay comfortably within that circle. "If they're anywhere to the northward of this, we can agree we've slipped past them already."

In the War Room a smaller circle was being swept out on a chart, the new outermost of a series of concentric circles surrounding *Bismarck's* last known position.

"That's her 'farthest on' now, sir," said a young officer, "assuming her speed constant."

"And the Home Fleet's heading northeastward?" said the admiral.

"Yes, sir. That's their track, as close as we can estimate."

The line, which all day yesterday had steadily converged towards the line of the *Bismarck's* track, now swerved

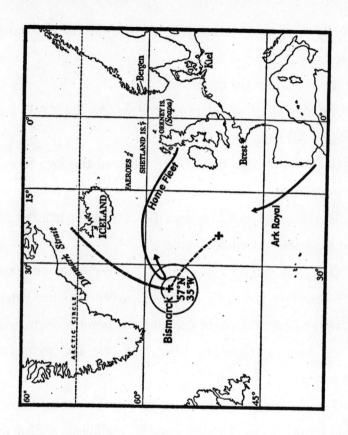

Map 6

". . . Home Fleet's heading northeastward?"

directly away from it, heading towards the eastern shore of Iceland.

"Nothing from the air at all?"

"Nothing at all, sir. Here are the sweeps the R.A.F. are making. All negative."

On another chart, dotted lines showed the area swept by the planes.

"Then it looks as if *Bismarck* didn't turn northeastward, and we guessed wrong. A pity."

"I'd hardly call it certain yet, sir," said the rear admiral.

"Remember the Chiefs of Staff agreed that the worst thing the *Bismarck* could do, from our point of view, was to get back to Germany unscathed. We had to guard against it—and we did."

"Yes. It doesn't follow, though, that the enemy knows what we think would be the worst . . . . Supposing, *Bismarck* headed for Brest the moment *Suffolk* lost her, where'd she be now?"

A dotted line was ruled out to the circle's circumference

from the center.

"THERE, sir."

"And the Home Fleet's THERE?"

"Yes, sir."

"Then it looks as if *Bismarck*'s given us the slip. The Home Fleet can't catch her if she once gets ahead."

"Unless something happens to slow her up, sir."

"Yes. There's *Ark Royal . . .* " said the admiral, tapping the chart with his forefinger.

The Swordfish pilots of the *Ark Royal* were sitting in the operations room before the blackboard being briefed regarding the situation.

"Now you can see how it is. The worst thing *Bismarck* can do, as far as we can see, is to escape back the way she came. The Home Fleet's been moving to cut her off, whether she goes past Iceland to the east or to the west. Besides that, she could have turned northwestwards, round the back side of Greenland—it's a likely area for a rendezvous with tankers. Or she could head southwestwards, just outside the limit of air search from Canada. *Revenge,* from Halifax, may have a chance then. Or she can head directly south; she could have a rendezvous with tankers off the Azores beyond our limits of air search there. *Ramillies* and *Edinburgh* will attend to that. Or she may be heading for the Mediterranean, or a Spanish port, or a French port—Brest or St. Nazaire. And that's where we come in, gentlemen. That's our job, if she comes this way. We have to find her, and then we have to put enough torpedoes into her at least to slow her down for the other forces to finish her off. *Our* torpedoes, gentlemen."

Farther along on the same deck, Ginger was instructing a new draft on the management and maintenance of torpedoes.

"Well, now you've seen all the works, you young sprogs. Maybe if this war goes on another five years or so you'll know something about the care and maintenance and lubrication of torpedoes. But there's one thing for you to get into your heads now: We—you and me—*we* win wars. Yes, you and me. These things"—slapping a torpedo—"sink ships. There's Winston in London. He knows what's wanted. There's the admiral, he makes plans. There's James Somerville with his admiral's flag. He commands Force H. There's Captain Maund of this ship. You all know what he does. There's the young officers of the Fleet Air Arm. They fly off and drop the torpedoes. But it's us that really count. Us, you and me. For if those torpedoes don't run straight and maintain a proper depth, and if they don't keep that up without varying a foot either way in three miles—well, then the torpedoes miss. And in that case, Winston and the admiral and James Somerville and Captain Maund and the Fleet Air Arm might just as well have stayed at home for all the good they've done. You just keep that in mind if ever you feel like saying 'That'll do. That's good enough.' It's hits that win wars, and it's us that makes the hits."

For one whole endless gray day ships were plunging across

the wide Atlantic, the *King George V* and the *Rodney,* Force H and Vian's destroyers; and planes flew perilously below the clouds to comb the surface, all searching for the *Bismarck.* And *Bismarck* remained lost. The neutral press, the American papers, all speculated about it. "Has *Bismarck* escaped?" they asked. Even in the English papers there were headlines like QUESTIONS TO BE ASKED IN THE HOUSE. People in factory canteens were saying over cups of coffee: "It'll be too bad if they lose her."

In the chartroom of the *King George V* a good many sleeves bearing plenty of gold lace were visible round a table while the fleet navigating officer demonstrated on the chart.

"Here's *Bismarck's* last known position and here's her 'farthest on.' It's a pretty big circle by now, I'm afraid. She could be anywhere inside that, and it's as big as all Europe by now. *But* . . . There have been air searches HERE"—the navigating officer rapidly covered one area with parallel lines—and HERE, and HERE."

A peculiar significance was instantly apparent. A full half of the circle was covered by the parallel lines.

"We've followed this course with a screen twenty miles wide, so this area here is accounted for, too. You can see what's left.

"If he hasn't headed straight south there's only one thing he could have done. Headed for France."

The moment the chart was marked in that way the truth of what was being said was apparent.

"And then he'd be THERE," said another voice, and an arm with an admiral's gold lace reached forward.

"I'm afraid so, sir."

"A hundred miles ahead of us, and he's faster than we are."

"I'm afraid that's true, too, sir. They couldn't search everywhere. Not enough planes, weather too bad, everything of that sort."

"I hope at least they're searching this area now. Where's *Ark Royal?* She ought to be near enough now to search

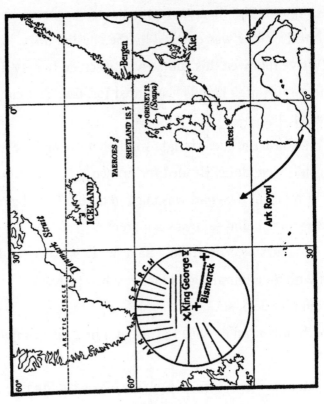

Map 7

". . . only one thing he could have done. Headed
for France."

from the south."

"Here she is, sir, by the Admiralty appreciation."

Ark Royal was enduring appalling weather. She was plunging over the waves so that when she turned into the wind her bows and her stern were rising and falling fifty feet at a single plunge. It was raining and bitterly cold as the Swordfish were ranged on the flying deck. It was only with the utmost difficulty that the planes were able to take the air, to fly off on their search. They vanished instantly into the grayness.

And elsewhere Catalinas had taken off from Lough Erne in Ireland to search in a southwesterly direction, flying through the night so as to be over their search area by daylight. Southwesterly they flew, on parallel courses far out of sight of each other, turning as they reached the limits set for the search, flying fifty miles northwest, and then turning northeasterly to fly back, covering a wide area of the ocean with their tracks as with a gridiron—a gridiron which was being drawn upon the chart in the War

Room, a fresh bar being added, a new line being drawn, as each turn was reported by wireless. The area on the chart uncovered by air or sea search was steadily dwindling. And a Catalina was nearly at the limit of its endurance when the crew saw something below.

"What's that?" demanded someone.

The weather was so thick that they were flying only five hundred feet above the tossing water. Yet even so the vessel they saw was vague and undefined. They were almost above it.

"Get closer! Get round its stern," said the man in the second pilot's seat.

"That's a battleship. And no destroyer screen . . . That's the *Bismarck!*"

The observer grabbed a form and began to write out a signal. Even as he did so, the Catalina jolted and jerked as a shell burst close alongside. As he went on writing the pilot turned the plane frantically; the sea and the ship below wheeled in a circle as she came round, with shellbursts all round her, and climbed for cloud cover. As the mist closed round her the wireless operator began to tap out the message.

Admiral Lutjens was asleep in his armchair, his head on his hand, when the alarm blared out throughout the ship. He awoke with a start, blinked himself alert, and rushed for the bridge. All over the ship the alarm awoke sleeping figures, exhausted men lying uncomfortably on the decks or sitting against bulkheads, sleeping uneasily while the rest strove to keep themselves awake at their posts, dirty and bearded and untidy, sometimes even nodding off, until the alarm blared.

"Plane on the port bow! Plane on the port bow!"

The AA guns wheeled about, pointed for a moment, and then burst into rolling thunder as the shells were hurled at the Catalina. Lutjens and Lindemann met on the bridge.

"Well, Captain, they've found us at last."

"Yes, sir. That was a Catalina—a shore-based plane, sir."

"Yes."

They entered the chartroom.

"How close to France can we expect air cover from the Luftwaffe?" demanded Lutjens.

The navigator drew a circle on the chart, and shaded in the area between it and the French shore.

"That's the approximate line, sir." He swung the dividers between the marked position of the *Bismarck* and the edge of the circle. "And we shall reach there at dawn tomorrow, sir."

Lutjens and Lindemann eyed each other.

"Dawn tomorrow," said Lindemann, looking at the clock. "Ten more hours of daylight today . . . "

"And then we'll have air cover," said Lutjens. "Then nobody will dare to touch us."

The wireless officer appeared and saluted. "We're taking in the British plane's signals, sir," he said.

"Can you read them?"

"Not in that code, sir. But the form's clear enough. Our position, course, and speed."

"I didn't think it would be Christmas greetings," said Lutjens.

"And we have picked up two other brief signals, sir."

"Well?"

"I could not read them either, sir. But I could recognize who were transmitting, Swordfish, sir."

"Swordfish?" This was an exclamation from Lindemann.

"Yes, sir."

"Thank you, Lieutenant," said Lutjens.

The wireless officer withdrew and they bent over the chart.

"A carrier means Force H from Gibraltar," said Lutjens. "That can easily be in this area. What's their possible position? You know when they sailed."

The navigator swept another circle, centering on Gibraltar. It passed close to *Bismarck*'s marked position.

"They can be in touch with us at any moment, sir," said the navigator.

The chief of staff flipped open a reference book of profiles.

"Force H," he said, showing one: *"Renown."*

"Five minutes' work for our guns."

"Sheffield."

"She wouldn't risk a single salvo from us."

"Ark Royal."

"It's her Swordfish that we can hear. We've beaten off one attack by Swordfish already. There's nothing to frighten us in the prospect of another."

During this conversation the navigator had fallen asleep with his head resting on his hand, to be roused as his elbow slipped on the table.

"Except that nobody in this ship has been to bed for six days and six nights, sir," said Lindemann.

"Only one more night now, Lindemann. Only one more night."

They went out onto the bridge again and looked over the heaving sea.

"A rough sea, low cloud, visibility as bad as possible.

Not the conditions for an aircraft carrier," said Lutjens.

In the *Ark Royal* Ginger's working party were busy putting a torpedo into position in a Swordfish. An officer checked it over.

"Magnetic pistol, sir," said Ginger.

"Very good."

They wheeled the Swordfish forward into position. Wind was blowing and spray was flying.

In the operations room in *Ark Royal* it was obvious that it was a rough sea. Everything was pitching and saying as the pilots were being finally briefed.

"There it is, gentlemen," said the senior observer. "You have *Bismarck*'s position, course and speed. Our shadowers are over her. The rest of it is up to you. Your torpedoes have the new magnetic pistols, which may help. Unless you stop her, unless you slow her up, she's safe. Tomorrow morning she'll be under air cover. Nine hours of daylight left. The Home Fleet's a hundred miles astern of her and can never catch her in time. So you know where your duty lies, gentlemen. And good luck go with you."

In the War Room at the Admiralty a rather depressed group of officers was standing watching the chart being brought up to date.

"Ten hours more of daylight," said the rear admiral. "Big sea running and low cloud."

"Coastal Command's coming through on the 'phone, sir," said an officer. "Yes. Repeat that. 40° 30 North, 22° West, steering 150°. Yes . . . . Catalina reports a battleship, sir."

He spoke to deaf ears, for everyone was at the chart. Someone marked the place, almost in the center of the triangle, whose angles were the *King George V, Rodney,* and *Ark Royal.*

"Must be *Bismarck.* Can't be anything else," said the rear admiral. "She's been heading for France ever since we lost her."

"What are those distances?" snapped the admiral.

"A hundred and forty miles for *King George V*. A hundred and thirty for *Rodney,* sir."

"They can't catch her there. No chance at all."

"Unless *Ark Royal* slows her up, sir."

"Yes. I know. That's the chance, for what it's worth. And there's Vian's five destroyers. They can intercept after nightfall. I know."

The Admiral's voice was flat and without tone. But was instantly full of energy again. "See that report's sent out instantly."

"It's going out now, sir," said the officer.

"Ten hours of daylight. Nine and a half," said the admiral, looking at the clock.

"Plenty of time for an attack by *Ark Royal*'s Swordfish," said the rear admiral.

"Wind's due west. She'll have to turn out of her course to fly off and fly on."

"Yes. She'll have time for one daylight attack. She'll be

lucky if she has time for two before dark."

"And after dark?"

"Not so good, I'm afraid."

"There's still the destroyers, sir," said another hopeful officer.

"A high sea and a battleship going 27 knots. How much chance?"

"Well—"

"How much?"

"Not very much, I'm afraid, sir. Unless she's crippled."

"So we come back to the *Ark Royal* again."

The meeting seemed about to break up when a Captain E. came up with a paper in his hand.

"Here area the fuel consumption figures for *King George V* and *Rodney,* sir, as close as I can calculate them. They're not too good, sir."

"Fuel?"

Down in the depths of *King George V.* Lieutenant Commander E., with a petty officer and a stoker were sounding the fuel tanks, going from one to another, hauling out the dipstick, wiping it, dropping it in again, and then hauling it out for inspection. At each sight the Lieutenant Commander E. made a noncommittal noise and note the figure on a piece of paper. On every dipstick there was only a very little oil apparent, at the very end.

"That one's dry, sir," said the petty officer at one inspection.

"Very well," said the Lieutenant Commander E., and went into the engine room where the bright lights shone and the engines sang their song and the Commander E. stood watching, in his boiler suit. The lieutenant commander shook his head as he came up.

"Not a hope, sir," he said. "Here's the figures."

Commander E. took the list and nodded agreement as he looked at the total.

"You know *Bismarck*'s been found?"

"Where is she, sir?"

"She's a hundred and forty miles right ahead of us. Going straight for France."

"That's bad, isn't it?"

"At top speed we couldn't catch her, and she'll reach Brest this time tomorrow."

"Well—"

"And by daylight she'll be within range of air cover. The whole Luftwaffe will be over her."

"Yes, I suppose so."

"Oh, what's the use of talking about it, anyway?" said the Commander E. in sudden fury. "We can't steam all-out for four hours, let alone twenty-four. At economical speed we can just get home, even if we can do that. Our destroyers have gone home for lack of oil, and now . . . Oh . . . !"

On the bridge of the *Bismarck,* Lutjens and Lindemann stood watching the ship plunge and toss in the appalling weather.

"You must remember the enemy has his troubles, too, Captain," said Lutjens. "He must be boiling with rage at this very moment now that he knows where we are. Now that we've broken through the ring with a clear run for home."

"A clear run except for the Swordfish, sir. We're picking up the shadowers' reports all the time."

Round the ship could be seen men carrying food to the men at their posts. They had to shake those men who were being allowed to sleep so as to rouse them to take their food, and even then it was received without appetite and allowed to lie neglected while the ship heaved and tossed over the strong sea.

"I think I had better address the ship's company," said Lutjens.

He went to the loud speaker, was announced by the petty officer there, and began:

"Men of the *Bismarck! Heil Hitler!* I am addressing you once more, and I think it will be for the last time, for the last time until we are back in port. You know we are being shadowed by planes from the *Ark Royal*. We are taking in their reports. Soon we must expect an attack to be launched against us. Swordfish with torpedoes. We've fought Swordfish before, as you remember, and we've nothing to fear from them, as long as we all do our duty, every one of us. Whatever attack they launch, we must beat off. I know you are tired, men of the *Bismarck*. I know you are sleepy. But I promise you that you have only this one effort more to make. Tomorrow morning we shall be within range of the Luftwaffe, and no Swordfish will dare to take the air within fifty miles of us. Tomorrow night you will sleep in peace. You will sleep undisturbed. That I promise you. Until then, fight on for the honor of the German Navy, for the greater German State, and for our Führer. *Heil Hitler!*"

The signal officer was waiting for him as he turned away from the loud speaker.

"I've just picked up a curious signal, sir."

"What?"

"From a British ship, and I think from the carrier *Ark*

Royal, sir."

"Well?"

"It was not in code. It was being sent very urgently in plain English."

"Well, what was it, man?"

"It said: LOOK OUT FOR *Sheffield.* LOOK OUT FOR *Sheffield.* Over and over again, sir."

"*Sheffield.* That's the cruiser with Force H," said the chief of staff.

"What was I just saying to you, captain?" said Lutjens. "The English are having their troubles, too."

"But—"

"If that message, whatever it means, was urgent enough to be sent in plain English, it shows they're having trouble. And I don't think we're sorry, are we?"

In Force H the senior observer was saying his last words to the pilots.

"*Bismarck*'s now twenty-four miles from us, bearing

183º. You can't miss her. You can't mistake her. She's all by herself. Don't give her a moment's warning—but I don't have to give you that sort of instruction. We'll be turning into the wind in five minutes' time."

Commander Air on the wing of the bridge looked in and reported, "Ready to fly off, sir." The *Ark Royal* turned solemnly into the wind as the order was passed down the voice-pipe from the bridge, and she was held exactly in position with the indicators showing that this was so. The fifteen Swordfish flew off in accordance with the orders given on the flight deck. They formed up and dashed away.

The signal officer came running frantically to the bridge where the captain stood with the officer of the watch.

"*Sheffield*'s over there too, sir. She's in visual touch and she turned out of line on an opposite course to us when we turned into the wind."

"*Sheffield*'s there?" said the captain.

"Yes, sir, and the Swordfish pilots have instructions to attack any ship they find alone."

"Send LOOK OUT FOR *Sheffield* to them. Quick! Send in plain language—don't waste a second!"

"Aye aye, sir."

The first Swordfish was flying in cloud when the observer picked up a pip on the radar. He advised the pilot who put down the nose of the plane and swept out into the clear, steadied for the aim, dropped his torpedo, and wheeled away. The second followed him and did the same; so did the third. But the pilot of the third, to his surprise, saw the first two torpedoes exploding in great fountains of water after running almost no distance. The fourth one followed him and dropped his torpedo. At that moment the gunner in the fifth one heard a signal in his ear-phones and scribbled a frantic message and passed it to the observer:

LOOK OUT FOR *Sheffield.*

The observer frantically called the pilot's attention to it at the moment when he was about to drop his torpedo.

The pilot drew his hand back hastily and wheeled the Swordfish round. The others followed him.

The whole flight circled back to come onto *Ark Royal* again, back onto the heaving deck, where eager crews awaited them, to rearm them while the air crews gathered in the briefing room.

"Yes, it went wrong," said the Commander Air. "Now we've agreed about it. We have to remember this, so that it can't ever happen again; but let's forget it for today. Now we try again, the way we do in the Navy. There's just enough time for one more daylight attack. Yes, Mr. Jones?"

"Don't let's have any more magnetic pistols on the torpedoes, sir. They went off prematurely, the ones we dropped."

"I bet *Sheffield*'s not sorry, either," said another pilot.

"That's something gained from the mess, anyway," said the Commander Air. "We know we can't rely on magnetic exploders. My guess is it was the rough sea that set 'em off. I'm having contact pistols put in the torpedoes at this very moment."

That was what Ginger and his party were doing; removing a magnetic pistol from a torpedo and substituting a contact pistol.

"This is where we win the war, you lads and me," said Ginger, working carefully on the job. "This thing's got to go off when it hits the *Bismarck,* and not before and not after. Otherwise we might just as well invite Hitler into Buckingham Palace this evening. That's it. Now bring the perisher along."

On the flight deck the torpedo on its trolley was hard to manage as the ship surged over the waves. But it was placed in position under the Swordfish at last, and the fifteen planes were ranged ready to take off. Commander Air reported this on the bridge and the ship turned into the wind again.

"An hour of daylight left," said the Commander Air to the captain.

"Those boys mean business," said the captain, and the

Swordfish droned on their way.

"There's not another ship in the world," said the Commander Air, "that could have flown planes off and on in these conditions."

In the *Bismarck*, Lutjens and Lindemann were looking at the gray sky.

"They should have attacked two hours ago," said Lindemann.

"One of the unpredictable accidents of war, I expect," said Lutjens. "One more hour of daylight . . . That's all."

At this moment came the yell of "Plane on the starboard bow!" followed by the roar of the alarm. The AA guns turned and began to fire, but the deafening racket was pierced by further cries: "Plane on the port beam. Plane on the starboard quarter."

Lindemann was giving rapid help orders, which transmitted down the voice-pipe, were translated into violent action by the helmsman at the wheel. The ship turned and twisted, to leave behind her a boiling, curved wake. There was a crash and a great jet of water at the bow as one torpedo exploded there; but the ship fought on without apparent damage. Then came a Swordfish, swooping at the stern as she sung; the wake of her dropped torpedo was clearly visible. On the wing of the bridge, Lutjens was shaking his fists at the plane.

"Hard-a-port. Hard-a-port!" shouted Lindemann, but there was not time to check the turn. The torpedo hit on her swinging stern, bursting close by the rudder in a shower of spray. A frightful vibration made itself felt throughout the ship, as if the whole vast structure would shake itself to pieces, and she heeled over madly as she continued in a tight turn.

"Starboard! Starboard!" shouted Lindemann.

Down below, the helmsman was struggling with the wheel while the compass before him still went swinging round over the card.

"I can't move the wheel, sir!" he said. "Rudder's

jammed!"

On the bridge the vibration still continued and the ship still circled. A telephone squawked and the officer of the watch answered it.

"Engine room, sir," he said to the captain.

"Captain," said Lindemann calmly into the telephone. "Yes . . . . Yes . . . . Very well."

The shattering vibration ceased as he hung up, and some of th speed of the ship fell away.

"Portside engines stopped, sir," he said to the admiral. "Portside propellers were thrashing against some obstruction."

"Yes," said Lutjens.

Another telephone was squawking.

"Damage Control, sir," said the officer of the watch.

"Captain," said Lindemann into the telephone. "Yes . . . . Yes . . . . Very well, get going on that."

Then he turned to Lutjens.

"Steering flat is flooded, sir. Steering engine out of action."

"What about the hand steering?"

"They've just been trying it, sir, but the rudder's jammed right over. They're trying to clear it now."

"The fate of the Reich depends on getting that rudder clear," said Lutjens.

In the War Room in London the senior officers were gathered round a chart of a different sort. This was on a scale so large that it showed mostly blank ocean, with only a hint of the coast of France and Spain on the right-hand side. But pinned upon the blank area were several tabs, marked, conspicuously, *Bismarck, King George V, Rodney,* FORCE H, VIAN'S DESTROYERS; and leading up to each tab were the black lines of the tracks of those ships during the last several hours. The only other feature of the map was a wide arc of a circle marking the limit of air cover from France.

A junior officer came over with a message in his hand.

"*Sheffield* has *Bismarck* in sight now, sir," he said, making an adjustment to *Bismarck*'s position. "She's reporting position, course and speed."

"How long before she's under air cover now?" demanded the admiral.

Someone swept with his dividers from *Bismarck*'s position to the arc. "A hundred and seventy-two miles, sir."

"Less than seven hours before she's safe!" said the rear admiral.

"And only an hour of daylight. What the devil's *Ark Royal* up to?"

"Here's a most immediate signal coming through now, sir," said an officer, "from *Sheffield:* HAVE SIGHTED SWORDFISH ATTACKING. Bismarck FIRING."

"That's *Ark Royal*'s planes," said the admiral.

"Come on, men! Come on!" said the air vice marshal.

"Most immediate from *Sheffield* again: *Bismarck* CIRCLING."

"That's something gained, anyway," said the rear admiral.

"Not enough to matter," said the admiral.

"Most immediate from *Sheffield:* ATTACK APPARENTLY COMPLETED. SWORDFISH RETURNING."

The rear admiral began to speak, but the admiral checked him, as the officer was still speaking.

"*Bismarck* STILL CIRCLING."

"Then the attack's not over," said the rear admiral.

"There's something odd," said the admiral.

The signals were clattering down the tubes to be opened hastily, but they were all, clearly, merely confirmations of what the young officer was announcing from his telephone.

"*Bismarck* HEADING NORTH."

"Heading north? Heading *north?* That's straight for *Rodney*," said the admiral.

"Perhaps she's still avoiding a plane *Sheffield* can't see," said the rear admiral.

"I wonder . . . " said the admiral.

"ESTIMATE *Bismarck's* SPEED AT 10 KNOTS."

"That hardly sounds likely," said the admiral.

"It must be pretty well dark there now."

Another young officer at the telephones spoke:

"Most immediate signal coming through from *Ark Royal,* sir."

"It's time we heard from her."

"FIRST FIVE AIRCRAFT RETURNING REPORT NO HITS."

The air vice marshal struck his fist into his hand, but the message went on.

"SHADOWING AIRCRAFT REPORTS *Bismarck* COURSE NORTH, SPEED 9 KNOTS."

"Something's happened to her, for sure," said the admiral.

"AIRCRAFT REPORTS HIT ON *Bismarck's* STARBOARD BOW."

"Good! Good!" said the air vice marshal.

"But that wouldn't account for it," said the rear admiral.

"*Sheffield* reporting, sir," said the first young officer: "*Bismarck* COURSE NORTH, SPEED 9 KNOTS."

"There's no doubt about it, then," said the rear admiral.

"*Ark Royal* reporting, sir," said the second officer; "AIRCRAFT REPORTS HIT ON *Bismarck* RIGHT AFT."

"That's it, then!" said the rear admiral.

"Yes, that's it. Propellers or rudder, or both," said the admiral.

"*Bismarck* COURSE NORTH, SPEED 10 KNOTS."

"There's a heavy sea running and she can't turn her stern to it," said the admiral.

"Vian'll be up to her in an hour," said the rear admiral. "He'll keep her busy during the night."

"And *King George V* and *Rodney* will be up to her by daylight," said the admiral. "I think we've got her. I think we have."

"Hooray!" said the air vice marshal again.

"*Sheffield* reporting, sir: HAVE SIGHTED VIAN'S DESTROYERS

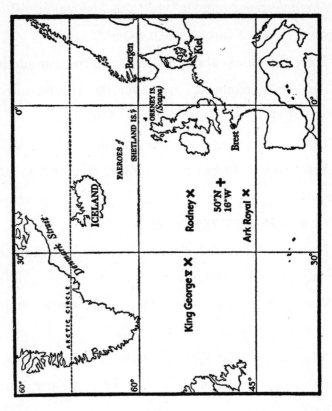

Map 8

"I think we've got her."

PREPARING TO ATTACK."

"Hooray!" said the air vice marshal again.

"Many men are going to die very soon," said the admiral.

"Any orders for Captain Vian, sir?"

There was only a moment's pause before that question was answered.

"No," said the admiral. "We all know Vian, and he knows his business. He won't lose touch with her. If she stays crippled he won't have to force the pace too much—he can bring in the battleships to get her at dawn. If she manages to repair herself he'll have to attack all-out."

"No so easy with that sea running," said the rear admiral. "And *Bismarck*'s got a good radar, apparently. The darkness will hamper him and won't hamper her."

"That won't stop Vian from attacking," said the rear admiral. "*Bismarck* is certainly going to have a lively night."

"All the better for our battleships tomorrow, then. Her

crew must be worn out already, and another sleepless night . . . But I'm not going to count our chickens before they're hatched. We don't know *all* that's going on."

Deep down in the stern of the *Bismarck* all was dark except for the beams of electric hand lamps. There was the sound of water washing back and forth, and the gleam of it, reflected from the lamps, came and went. The working party there was faintly visible. For a few seconds could be see a man in emergency diving kit disappearing into the surging water. A little farther forward a seaman was stringing an emergency wire which brought light to the dark spaces, so that now the dark water was illuminated as the sea surged backward and forward, roaring through the incredible confusion of twisted steel. There were pumps at work as the diver emerged, blood streaming from his lacerated shoulders. He made his report to the officer there, who went back to use the telephone against a dark bulkhead; to reach these a watertight door was opened for him and shut behind him, although, before it closed, the water came pouring in over the coaming with the movement of the ship. A working party was laboring to shore up the bulkhead, and he had to sign to the men to cease their deafening labor before he could make himself understood at the telephone switchboard.

In the chartroom of the *Bismarck* the captain was receiving the message.

"Yes," he said. "Yes. Very well."

Then when he replaced the telephone he addressed Lutjens and the staff officers gathered there.

"They don't think any repair can be effected," he went on. "Furthermore, unless we keep our bows to the sea they think the bulkhead will give way, and flood the next series of compartments. So we must hold this course as best we can."

"That means we go forward to meet our fate instead of trying to run away from it," said Lutjens. "That is what our Führer would like."

The chief of staff came forward with a bunch of signal forms in his hand.

"Berlin has just sent in a long message, a résumé of all the intelligence they can gather," he said. "The *King George V* is some fifty miles from us now, bearing northwesterly."

The assistant chief of staff opened the reference book to display a series of pictures.

"Fourteen-inch guns, speed 28 knots, 35,000 tons. Completed last year. Admiral Tovey's flagship; Captain Patterson."

"*Renown* and *Ark Royal*—"

"That's Force H," said Lutjens. "We know about them."

"And there's a force of destroyers, probably under Captain Vian—the man who captured the *Altmark*—close to us to the northward. From the position Berlin gives, they ought to be in sight now."

"No doubt they soon will be," said Lutjens. "I was hoping we might have a quiet night before our battle tomorrow."

"The men are falling asleep at their posts, as you know,

sir," said Lindemann.

"Yes," said Lutjens.

"And there's the *Rodney*," went on the chief of staff. "She's in touch with the *King George V*, and may even have joined her by now."

The assistant chief of staff opened the reference book at another page. "Sixteen-inch guns, speed 24 knots, 35,000 tons, completed soon after the last war. Captain Dalrymple Hamilton."

"Twenty years old," said Lutjens. "And I know her well. I lunched on board her in '24 at Malta when I was a young lieutenant."

It called for no effort on the part of Lutjens to conjure up the memory before his mind's eye. The heat and the dazzling sunshine and the smooth water of the harbor—all so different from this bitter cold and tossing sea and gray sky—and the spotless battleship, glittering with fresh paint and polished brasswork; the white handropes, the white uniforms, the dazzling gold lace; the bosun's mates lined up with their calls to their lips; the welcoming group of officers on the quarterdeck as Lutjens followed his captain on board; the salutes and the handshakes, the introductions and the formalities, before the English captain led the way below to a wide airy cabin, the armchairs gay with chintz, the table covered with white linen, the glassware sparkling.

"That was the peacetime navy," said Lutjens.

If Lutjens could have seen the *Rodney* now, as she plowed over the sea towards him, he would hardly have recognized her. A British lieutenant and an American naval lieutenant were at that moment on the boat deck of the *Rodney* looking around them at the ship.

"A battle's the last thing we expected," said the Englishman.

"That's what it looks like," said the American.

His eyes traveled over the boat deck and the upper deck. They were piled with wooden cases secured in every available space.

"This Lend-Lease of yours," said the Englishman. "Very kind of you to refit us, I know. We couldn't do without it. But we have to bring half our refitting stores with us, the things you can't supply because of our different standards."

"I know about that," said the American.

"Those are pom-pom mountings," said the Englishman.

"They look more like the Pyramids," said the American. They were eyeing at the moment two enormous wooden cases that towered up beside them on the boat deck.

"We've five hundred invalids on board for Canada," went on the Englishman. "They'll see another battle before they see Canada, anyway, and their wishes haven't been consulted about it."

"Me too," replied the American mildly. "I'm only supposed to be quietly showing you the way to Boston."

"That's the old *Rodney* for you," said the Englishman. "She can't even start off on a quiet trip to America without crossing the bows of a German battleship. We always try to do our guests well—entertainment regardless of expense.

You'll see fireworks tomorrow."

"Very kind of you," said the American.

"Mind you," went on the Englishman, "it may not be quite as lavish as we'd like. We haven't had time for a refit for two years. We're old and we're dingy. But we'll show you something good tomorrow, all the same. When those fellows talk—"

He pointed down to the turrets where the main armament crews were exercising. It was a moment of indescribable menace, as the sixteen-inch guns trained and elevated.

That was the same moment that Admiral Lutjens looked round at the rather depressed faces all round him, and went on: "Now, gentlemen, there's no need to despair. Three days ago we fought two battleships and won a tremendous victory. Now we face two battleships again. Our fighting capacity is unimpaired. We can sink this *King George V* and this Admiral Tovey. We can make this *Rodney* run away like the *Prince of Wales*. By noon tomorrow there'll be such an assembly of U-boats around us that no one will dare to attack us. We aren't fighting a battle of despair. We're fighting for victory. And for the German Navy, the Reich, and the Führer!"

It appeared as if his fighting words had some effect. Heads were raised higher again, and there was animation in the faces of those he addressed. Lindemann looked at the clock.

"Another half-hour of daylight," he said. "I'll have food issued to the men while there's time, before we darken ship."

"Always the thoughtful officer, Lindemann," said Lutjens.

And so the last meal was served out and carried round to the men at their posts during the last minutes of daylight. There were men who went on sleeping—men of that half of the crew who were allowed to sleep after the alarm of the attack by the Swordfish had ended, who flung themselves down on the steel decks in their aching longing for sleep. There were men who took a few mouthfuls of food. There were men who ate eagerly, with appetite. And there were the men struggling with damage repair below, who had no chance either to eat or sleep.

But darkness closed down form the gray sky so abruptly that even the half-hour of which Lutjens had spoken was cut short. The alarm roared through the ship. The sleepers whom even the alarm could not now rouse were shaken or kicked awake.

The voice pipe spoke abruptly to the group in the chartroom: *"Destroyer on the starboard bow"*—and directly afterwards: *"Destroyer on the port bow."*

Outside, the darkened ship was suddenly illuminated by the flash of the secondary armament. The guns bellowed. That was the beginning of a dreadful night. As the hands of the clock crept slowly round, alarm followed alarm. *"Destroyer to port!"* *"Destroyer to starboard!"*

In the outer blackness, Vian's five destroyers—four British and one Polish—had made their way to shadowing positions encircling the *Bismarck*. It was not so easy to do in that howling wind and over that rough sea. The destroyers that made their way to *Bismarck*'s port side had to head directly into the waves.

The captain and navigating officer on the bridge of the leading destroyer felt the frightful impact as the successive seas crashed upon the forecastle, and the spray that flew aft was so solid that it was impossible to see anything as they looked forward.

"We can't keep it up," said the captain. "Slow to 18 knots."

At that speed the destroyer could just withstand the battering of the seas—although the plight of the men in exposed situations was horrible—and she could go weaving and plunging forward. The lookouts straining their eyes through the darkness could see nothing, could not pick out the smallest hint of the vast bulk of the *Bismarck* battling the waves. The lookout peering over the starboard bow was conscious of nothing—strive as he would—except roaring darkness and hurtling spray. Yet as he watched, the darkness was suddenly rent by the long vivid flashes of gunfire—pointed, as it seemed to him, directly into his eyes. Four seconds later—no more—the howl of the wind was augmented by the scream of shells overhead; the sea all about the destroyer was torn into wilder confusion still by a hail of splashes, and plainly through the lurching and staggering of the ship could be felt the sharper impact of shell fragments against the frail hull.

"Port fifteen," said the captain, and the destroyer swung away abruptly. Before her turn was completed the long flashes of the *Bismarck*'s guns appeared again in the darkness, and close under the destroyer's stern the salvo plunged into the sea to raise splashes brief-lived in the brisk wind.

"Good shooting in the dark," said the captain.

"That's their radar."

The destroyer's turn had taken her into the trough of the sea, and now she was rolling fantastically, far over, first on one side and then on the other, as the steep waves heaved her over.

"We'll try again," said the captain. "Starboard fifteen."

Another series of long flames, but longer and brighter than the preceding ones, stabbed into the darkness over there, yet no salvo splashed about them.

"One of the others is getting it," remarked the navigator.

"That's their fifteen-inch," said the captain. "They're using their secondary armament for us and the main battery on the other side."

The destroyer put her nose into a sea and something much solider than spray came hurtling aft to cascade against the bridge.

"We can't take that," said the captain. "Turn two points to port and slow to 15 knots."

A few seconds after the order had been given the gun flashes lit the sky to starboard again, and close beside the starboard bow the salvo hit the water.

"Just as well we made that turn," said the captain "That's

good shooting."

"And we haven't even seen her yet!" marveled the navigator.

"They haven't seen us either," said the captain. "This is modern warfare."

It was modern warfare. Far down below decks in the *Bismarck,* walled in by armor plate, a group of officers and men sat at tables and switchboards. Despite the vile weather outside, despite the wind and the waves, it was almost silent in here; in addition to the quiet orders and announcements of the radar fire-control team there could only be heard the low purring of the costly instruments they handled. Centered in the room was the yellow-green eye of the radar, echoing the impressions received by the aerial at the masthead a hundred feet above; the room was half dark to enable the screen to be seen clearly. And in accordance with what that screen showed, dials were turned and pointers were set and reports were spoken into telephones; save for the uniforms, it might have been a gathering of medieval wizards performing some secret rite—but it was not the feeble magic of trying to cause an enemy to waste away by sticking pins into his waxen image or of attempting to summon up fiends from the underworld. These incantations let loose thousand foot tons of energy from the *Bismarck*'s guns and hurled instant death across ten miles of raging sea. It was a result of what that eye saw that the exhausted men of the *Bismarck* forced themselves into renewed activity to serve the guns, although there were actually men who fell asleep with the guns bellowing in their very ears. Now and then, a dazzling flash, star shells soared up from the destroyers and hung over the doomed battleship, lighting her up as if it were day. Sometimes there would be a shadowy glimpse of the destroyers racing to get into position, their bow-waves gleaming except when the heavy seas burst over their bows. Even Lutjens himself was overtaken by sleep as he sat in the control room, nodding off in his chair while the guns fired, and pulling himself up with a jerk. Once when he roused himself he called a staff officer to his side.

"Send this to Berlin at once. WE SHALL FIGHT TO THE LAST. LONG LIVE THE FÜHRER."

In the War Room in London the rear admiral entered after an absence.

"Vian's still engaging her," explained one of the officer.s

"*Bismarck*'s still transmitting," said another.

"What's the weather report?"

"No change, sir. Wind force 8, westerly. High sea running, low cloud, visibility poor."

"*King George V* will sight her soon enough."

Back in the control room of the *Bismarck,* Lutjens was nodding off again in his chair. His head sank lower and lower, and after a while he gave up the struggle and settled back into a sound sleep. It lasted very little time, however, because the chief of staff came to him and laid a hand on his shoulder.

"Sunrise in half an hour, sir."

"I shall go on the bridge," said Lutjens. "I think a breath of fresh air will do me good."

"Your overcoat, sir," said his flag lieutenant as he went out.

"Do you think I shall need it?" asked Lutjens, but he put it on nevertheless.

Outside, the faint light was increasing. As ever, the wind was shrieking round them; the ship was rolling heavily in the waves, with the spray flying in sheets.

"Good morning, Admiral," said Lindemann.

"Good morning, Captain," said Lutjens.

"Destroyers out of range on the starboard bow, sir," said Lindemann. "And there's a cruiser somewhere to the northward of us. I'm sure she's the *Norfolk.*"

"That was the ship that sighted us in Denmark Strait," said Lutjens. "Still with us, is she?"

One of the lookouts blinked himself awake and stared forward through his binoculars. "Ship right ahead! Two ships right ahead!"

Lutjens and Lindemann trained their glasses forward.

"Battleships?" asked Lutjens.

"I think so, sir. Battleships."

The lookout in *King George V* was staring through is glasses.

"Ship right ahead!"

"Ship bearing green 5!"

"That's *Bismarck!*" said an officer on the bridge of *Rodney.*

Down the voice pipe, over the head of the quartermaster at the wheel of the *Rodney,* came a quiet order.

"Port ten."

"Port ten, sir," repeated the quartermaster, turning his wheel.

Up in the gunnery control tower the captain's voice made itself heard in the gunnery officer's earphones.

"We are turning to port. Open fire when your guns bear."

The gunnery officer looked down at the GUN READY

lights. He looked through his glasses with the pointer fixed upon the silhouette of the *Bismarck.*

"Fire!" he said.

Out on the wing of the bridge stood the American officer and the British lieutenant, glasses to their eyes. Below them, just as on the evening before, the sixteen-inch guns were training round and reaching upwards towards extreme elevation. Then came the incredible roar and concussion of the salvo. The brown cordite smoke spurted out from the muzzles, to be borne rapidly away by the wind as the shells took their unseen way on their mission of death.

"Short but close. Damned close," said the Englishman; the last words were drowned by the din of the second salvo, and he did not speak again during the brief time of flight. But when he spoke it was in a voice high-pitched with excitement. "A hit! A hit! At the second salvo! I told you the old *Rodney*—"

Again his words were drowned by the roar of the guns,

and he forced himself to keep his glasses steady on the target. Next it was the American who spoke.

"Another hit," he said. "She doesn't stand a chance now."

Down in the radar room of the *Bismarck* the same disciplined team was still at work.

"Range seventeen thousand meters," said the rating at the screen.

There was a roar like thunder then, all about them, as the first salvo hit the *Bismarck*. The lights went out and came on, went out and came on, and the yellow-green eye of the radar screen abruptly went lifeless. The rating there reached for other switches, clicked them on and off; he tried another combination.

"Radar not functioning, sir," he announced.

"You've tried the after aerial?" asked the officer.

"Yes, sir. No result."

"No connection with gunnery control, sir," announced

another rating.

"No connection with—" began another rating, but another rolling peal of thunder cut off his words, and again the lights flickered. "No connection with the bridge, sir."

"Very well."

"No connection with the charthouse, sir."

"Very well."

The first wisps of smoke had begun to enter the radar room through the ventilating system. Wisp after wisp it came, seeping in thicker and thicker, swirling in, while the lights burned duller and duller. And peal after peal of thunder shook the whole structure, the shock waves causing the wreaths of smoke to eddy abruptly with each impact, and a section of paneling fell from the bulkhead with a sudden clatter. It was as if the witches' Sabbath in which they had been engaged had now roused the infernal forces for their own destruction. Throughout the doomed ship the lights were burning low and smoke was creeping in thicker and thicker.

In the War Room the young officer was repeating the messages heard on the telephone.

"Most immediate from *Norfolk*. *Rodney* HAS OPENED FIRE . . . . *King George V* HAS OPENED FIRE . . . . *Bismarck* IS RETURNING THE FIRE . . . . *Bismarck* HIT . . . . *BISMARCK* HIT AGAIN."

It was almost possible for the men listening in the War Room to visualize what was actually going on. As the *Bismarck* trained her guns round, she was surrounded by a forest of splashes from *Rodney*'s salvo, and before she could fire, the splashes from *King George V*'s salvo surrounded her. Hardly had her guns spoken before a shell hit the second turret from forward and burst with a roar and a billow of smoke. The blast and the fragments swept everywhere about the bridge. The fabric was left a twisted litter of stanchions, and lying huddled and contorted in it were a number of corpses, among them those of

Lindemann—conspicuous by its Knight's Cross—and of Lutjens.

The voice of the officer at the telephone went on describing what was going on. *"Bismarck* ON FIRE AFT . . . . *Bismarck* HIT . . . .*Bismarck* HIT . . . .*Bismarck's* FORE TURRET OUT OF ACTION." Another officer broke in.

"Ark Royal signaling sir: ALL PLANES AWAY."

"Ark Royal? I can't believe her planes will find anything to do. But quite right to send them in."

On the flight deck of the *Ark Royal* the sound of the gunfire was plainly to be heard, loudly, in the intervals of the Swordfish revving up their engines and taking off. Conditions were as bad as ever as the ship heaved and plunged in the rough sea under a lowering gray sky, yet somehow the lumbering aircraft managed to get away, and circle, and get into formation, and head northwards, low over the heaving sea and close under the dripping clouds. It was only a few seconds before the leader saw what he was looking for. There was a long bank of black smoke lying on the surface of the water, spreading and expanding from the denser and narrower nucleus to the northward, and it was towards that nucleus that he headed his plane.

"My God!" said the leader.

The smoke was pouring from the battered, almost shapeless hull of the *Bismarck,* stripped of her upper works, mast, funnels, bridge and all. Yet under the smoke, plainly in the dull gray light, he could see a forest—a small grove, rather—of tall red flames roaring upward from within the hull. But it was not the smoke nor the flames that held the eye, strangely enough, but the ceaseless dance of tall jets of water all about her. Two battleships were flinging shells at her both from their main and from their secondary armaments; and from the cruisers twenty eight-inch guns were joining in. There was never a moment when she was not ringed in by the splashes of the near-misses, but when the leader forced his eye to ignore the distraction of this wild water dance he saw something else: from bow to stern along the tortured hull he could see a continual coming and going of shellbursts, volcanoes of flame and smoke. From that low height, as the Swordfish closed in, he could see everything. He could see the two fore-turrets useless, one of them with the roof blown clean off and the guns pointing over side at extreme elevation, the other with the guns fore and aft drooping at extreme depression. Yet the aftermost turret was still in action; even as he watched, he saw one of the guns in it fling out a jet of smoke towards the shadowy form of the *King George V;* down there in the steel turret, nestling among the flames, some heroes were still contriving to load and train and fire. And he saw something else at the last moment of his approach. There were a few tiny, foreshortened figures visible here and there, scrambling over the wreckage, incredibly alive amid the flames and the explosions, leaping down from the fiery hull into the boiling sea.

He swung the Swordfish away from the horrible sight, to lead the way back to the *Ark Royal.* While that bombardment was going on there was no chance of a frail plane delivering a successful torpedo attack. He had seen the climax of the manifestation of sea power, the lone challenger overwhelmed by a colossal concentration of force. He was not aware of the narrowness of margin of time and space, of how in the British battleships the last few tons of oil fuel were being pumped towards the furnaces, of German U-boats hastening, just too late, from all points in the North Atlantic to try to intervene in the struggle, of German air power chafing at the bit unable to take part in a battle only a few miles beyond their maximum range.

While the squadron was being led back to the *Ark Royal,* the officer at the telephone in the War Room was continuing to announce the signals coming through.

"*Bismarck* HIT AGAIN . . . . SHE IS ONLY A WRECK NOW . . . . *King George V* AND *Rodney* TURNING AWAY."

In the War Room people looked sharply at each other at that piece of news. The admiral looked at the clock.